do-it-yourself
ADVERTISING

do-it-yourself
ADVERTISING
A Complete Action Guide

ROY BREWER

**KOGAN
PAGE**

First published in 1991

Apart from any fair dealing for the purposes of research or private
study, or criticism or review, as permitted under the Copyright,
Designs and Patents Act, 1988, this publication may only be
reproduced, stored or transmitted, in any form or by any means,
with the prior permission in writing of the publishers, or in the case
of reprographic reproduction in accordance with the terms of
licences issued by the Copyright Licensing Agency. Enquiries
concerning reproduction outside those terms should be sent to the
publishers at the undermentioned address:

Kogan Page Limited
120 Pentonville Road
London N1 9JN

© Roy Brewer 1991

British Library Cataloguing in Publication Data

A CIP record for this book is available from the British Library.

ISBN 0-7494-0211-3

Typeset by Saxon Printing Ltd, Derby
Printed and bound in Great Britain by
Biddles Limited, Guildford

Contents

Introduction

Please read this first

Advertising serves many users for many, and diverse, purposes, and calls on a wide range of specialisations and techniques. This book is intended for people who handle their own advertising, or wish to do so. It therefore concentrates on what is practicable within relatively limited resources.

Some £8.6 billion a year is spent on advertising in the UK. Though the total amount bought directly is far greater than that booked through agencies, the advertising expenditure of most individual advertisers is comparatively small. It is these for whom this book was written.

Advertising is not one huge industry, but rather a collection of interrelated communication systems, some more accessible and adaptable than others. So if the first question is 'Can I do it myself?' the reply must be 'It depends on what you want to do'. 'What can I do for myself?' is nearer to the question I have set out to answer; for unless a company has a substantial budget it probably has little choice but to handle its own advertising, using whatever resources it can command and whatever external services it can afford; and once it is accepted that advertising doesn't just happen, but has to be planned, created and produced, this can be done.

Advice and technical guidance can be given, but advertising cannot usually be done 'by the book' so, without saying 'Do it this way' – much less 'Do it *my* way' – it seemed sensible to apply my own knowledge and experience of the needs of smaller advertisers, who are frequently neglected in more ambitious and comprehensive studies. Some suggestions will call for examination in the cold light of available resources; but advertising is always worth what it costs in time, and effort and money to create if it secures the required response.

Though outdoor advertising, for example posters and illuminated displays, and television, film and broadcast advertising are important media, they are normally entirely agency booked and managed, and are therefore outside the scope of this book. I shall therefore be dealing mainly with print-based advertising, such as newspapers and magazines, direct mail, point of sale and brochures, which are more directly accessible and manageable by individual advertisers.

I will also be putting a good deal of emphasis on ideas – how you, the reader, can translate your specific needs into advertising concepts, in short how to think constructively about advertising. Internally, a company possesses a more detailed knowledge of its own products and services than anyone outside it, and this can be put to work in its advertising.

A logical sequence from planning, through creative work and media selection, to the production of finished advertisements has been attempted, but there are bound to be places where this will not apply and a direct route cannot be taken. In these cases cross-references in the text draw attention to relevant pages or chapters elsewhere in the book where additional information can be found.

Terms such as 'the company', 'products', 'services' and 'customers' are used simply to avoid awkwardness in the text. Advertising serves many users for many purposes: the advertising of a charitable organisation will obviously differ in important ways from that of a multiple store. This is not such a difficult problem as it seems. Every advertisement must first be noticed, then provide a convincing reason why the reader should respond as the advertiser wishes. These basic criteria are present in all advertising, whatever its content. If they can be met the advertising stands a chance. If they are misunderstood, or neglected, the cleverest, most expensively produced ad is a waste of money. It may be impossible to say *what* to advertise in a book like this and difficult to suggest *where* to advertise; but it is possible to explain *how* to advertise, whatever the reason for doing it.

Advertising jargon and technical terms are avoided wherever possible. Where there is likely to be any doubt about the meaning of a word I have used an easily understood equivalent in parenthesis.

The *action guides* contain brief, practical ideas and information which can be used as reference, or starting, points when read in conjunction with the more detailed discussion which precedes them.

The 'secret ingredients' of good advertising, imagination and enthusiasm, are for you to add. Good luck!

Roy Brewer
Clifton, Bristol
1991

CHAPTER 1
Making a Start

Planning

If it is not clear what's wanted from the outset it becomes increasingly difficult to discover whether advertising is producing satisfactory results and, if not, to know what can be done about it. Start with some really basic questions, even if you think you already know the answers: try to explain exactly *what* you advertise and *why* you advertise.

For present purposes we are concerned with objectives – how they might be reached can be left until later. Call it your advertising policy if you like, but 'advertising policy' is really only a fancy name for an advertising strategy, or plan. Circumstances may call for a change of plan, while a 'policy' suggests something rather less flexible. I have therefore called the three sections of this chapter – planning, costing and budgeting.

An advertising plan should be practicable. Keep it simple, work within your resources and base it on what you know, or can find out. At this stage it is more important to discover as much as possible about your company and what it is advertising than how you go about advertising it. That comes later.

One of the advantages of handling your own advertising is comparatively easy access to information unique to your company in such areas as marketing, product development and sales. Another is that, simply by making a plan, you are starting to think in practical terms about advertising, and discovering some things which will help you to tackle it more confidently and efficiently.

Here are some sample questions to ask yourself, and anybody else whose opinion you value:

- What, as well as products or services, are we selling?
- Do we know why our regular customers choose to buy from us rather than somebody else?
- Who and where are our existing customers, and how do we communicate with them?
- Who and where are our potential customers, and how can we reach them through our advertising?

It's easy to assume that the only reason for buying something is to acquire a particular product or service; but why yours rather than somebody else's? Maybe you give particularly reliable back-up, easier ordering or quicker delivery than your competitors. If so your advertising could benefit by featuring these strengths.

If, up to now, your company has done little advertising (or none at all) do not take anything for granted. Never mind, for the moment, what the experts say: advertising lore is full of wise saws, such as 'If you can invent a better mousetrap the world will beat a path to your door'. That implies that a good product sells itself; but, wait a minute! It's not much use inventing a better mousetrap if you don't tell anybody *why* it is better than the old sort . . . and, of course, where to find your door!

Techniques and skills – design, copywriting, artwork, presentation and production – are naturally important and I shall be dealing with these in due course; but, just as recipes alone do not make good cooks, all the technique in the world will not, on its own, produce successful advertising (as, indeed, even the professionals occasionally demonstrate!). There are no foolproof formulae in advertising.

Throughout the planning stages I cannot recommend too strongly the discipline of writing things down so that they can be examined, discussed and, if necessary, improved or amended. In this book I ask some questions which can only be answered satisfactorily from direct knowledge and experience. These are the important ones, because they concern *your* business, not that of some anonymous 'advertiser'. When you think you have reasonably satisfactory answers write them down, and be prepared to modify them in the light of experience. Remember, too, that though you are managing your advertising you simply cannot run the whole show on your own. Get used to taking advice and listening to what other people say, even if it isn't always what you would like to hear.

An advertising plan *must* be market orientated. Without market information advertising has to be conducted on a 'suck it and see' basis, which is fraught with dangers as well as being time-consuming and wasteful.

Action guide

- Write down what you already know, or can easily find out, about your company. Exactly what is it selling? Why do you think anybody buys it? It's not enough to say that you have a good, competitively priced product, or one which is better than your competitors'. In what *ways* is it good? In what *respects* do you believe it to be better? In price? Quality? Availability? Maybe in design or packaging. It's for you to say.

- What, in addition to a product or service, does your company offer? Promptness? Friendliness? Technical know-how? Convenience? Status? Fast delivery? *You* name it. If you're not sure canvass the opinions of sales staff, managers, suppliers, customers and anybody else who could help to reach an objective estimate of how your company conducts its business and serves its customers.

- What is known (or can reasonably be assumed) about your company's existing customers or clients? How are they distributed geographically? Into what income brackets, age ranges and social groups do they usually fall? Do most of them live in the UK or abroad, and where? In cities? In the country? Where are they likely to have seen or heard about you? In shops? In offices? In the street? At home? What newspapers and magazines are they likely to read?

- How much do you know about your competitors? In particular, what do you consider their strengths and weaknesses? Are they better situated, geographically, than you are to serve the market? Are they bigger or smaller than you? More or less efficient? Are their prices lower than yours? Is their advertising attractive? How much advertising do they do? How effective do you think it is?
- Now look critically at any advertising you have already undertaken. Did it produce the expected result, or don't you know? If it did can you say why?

This is a formidable raft of questions to which immediate answers may be difficult to find. Do not despair. An advertising plan gains in focus and realism with experience.

I have forgotten who said 'I waste half my money on advertising, but I'm never sure which half it is'. It sounds clever, but whoever it was must have had a great deal of money to be resigned to wasting 50 per cent of it on advertising. Advertising might look like 'bread on the waters', but if that is how it is seen and used you will need an awful lot of bread. The fact that there are no fixed rules does not mean there are no guidelines or precedents which can reduce the chances of errors and miscalculations. In later chapters I shall be suggesting ways of finding out more about how advertising works. There may be no guarantee that you will get what you want from advertising, but unless you know what you want there is no way of managing it.

So, for a start, be content to say as clearly and precisely as you can what you would like to achieve through your advertising. The following chapters will then help you to decide what resources you need to get it, and how to use them to get value for *more* than half the money you spend!

Costing

Without preliminary costing it is difficult to implement an

advertising plan. Costing precedes the setting of an advertising budget, for which it will be necessary to have more detailed information about what resources are available and how they could be allocated. Known costs, such as space rates, and some external services, such as printing and mailing, are fairly easily ascertained; but what the company will have to provide for itself – time, materials and other internal resources – also costs money.

A preliminary costing is an estimate of what you are likely to have to invest in a given amount of advertising. Without knowing, even approximately, what you are likely to spend on overheads it will be difficult to produce a realistic budget.

It is impossible to be dogmatic as to whether it is preferable to base the actual budget on a completed advertising schedule, or to allow the budget to control the schedule. Some compromises will almost certainly be necessary for, while it is not easy to allocate resources without an exact idea of what they will cost, it is equally difficult to adjust a worked-out schedule to an inflexible budget. This is why it is desirable to have a fair idea of what things cost before you attempt to create a budget.

Advertising attracts visible costs – space rates and overheads, such as services, materials, printing and mailing – and the invisible costs of managing, creative work and, perhaps, in-house origination. If expenditure is calculated solely on fixed costs there are likely to be unpleasant surprises. Costs change, space rates can go up or down. The aim is to arrive at a reasonably accurate estimate of everything you will need to undertake your planned advertising, otherwise you will not only be in the dark about prices but also unable to work out what return you are getting for your expenditure.

Existing expenditure, plus rate cards and enquiries, will help to establish the general cost structure of press media and production services. Additionally, if direct mail, sales letters, brochures and other in-house based activities are envisaged you should include the estimated cost to your company of such items as printing and distribution. How you evaluate the use of your own staff, equipment and services, such as word processors, photocopiers, telephone, fax, messengers, etc, is for you to decide, but you will know that these do not come free of charge!

Budgeting

A useful – though by no means foolproof – aid to setting a realistic advertising budget is first to calculate the net profit on each sale and multiply it by your sales turnover over a period comparable with that covered by your advertising budget. Remember that sales can be affected by seasonal and other variables. This could give you a reasonably realistic basis on which to work out what *proportion* of your existing profit could sensibly be devoted to advertising, ie what percentage of your net profit you are prepared to spend on advertising provided it can produce a sales increase.

You may have a fairly accurate idea from past experience of how much profit can be anticipated from advertising, though ultimately this will depend on such external factors as the size of the market and your potential share of it. Principally, it will rest on how well your advertising is conducted – there is no way round that – but provided your existing profit margin is maintained, and no increases in overhead costs such as labour and production are expected, the profit earned on each unit sold, less the cost of advertising, can be projected.

Let us take some straightforward instances, where advertising is carried out with the aim of producing direct sales and not, as it sometimes is, for other reasons. In this case the higher the net profit per unit the fewer sales will have to be made to cover the cost of advertising: 5 per cent of a profit of £1 per unit is 5p. Five per cent of a profit of £100,000 per unit is £5000. Which is the more likely for your particular product or service for each £1000 you plan to spend on advertising? In the former example £1000 of advertising would have to produce or maintain 2000 sales simply to break even, while in the latter a single additional sale produced or maintained by advertising would result in a £4000 profit.

The distinction between 'producing' and 'maintaining' sales is an important one. Some products rely wholly on advertising to produce sales, for example those offered exclusively through mail order catalogues. In this case the method is likely to be easy to apply. Others need advertising to *maintain* sales, eg theatres would not sell seats unless they advertised their productions. It can often be difficult to establish with certainty what proportion of sales can be directly assigned to advertising, and the 'profit/percentage' method will then be only a rough guide, but it's a start.

Crystal balls aside, basically what you are getting when you buy advertising is a 'platform' – a place from which to address a readership or an audience. How you use it is of little immediate concern to those who sell the platform: simply adding up what you pay for it does not determine how successful or otherwise your advertising will be. These are matters for later chapters. If you are still unsure about how to make an advertising budget skip the action guide for the moment and return to it later.

Action guide

- Budget for a specific period, say six months or a year.
- Base your budget on accurate, up-to-date information. Do not forget in-house costs, such as materials and postage, and bought-in services. Include any anticipated price increases. Try to arrive at a *total* costing for your projected advertising over the chosen period.
- Allocate your advertising expenditure intelligently and in accordance with what you already know, or can discover, about your markets and customers. For example, a budget divided into 12 equal monthly 'instalments' for a product with seasonal demand or availability would clearly not be realistic.
- Pay special attention to any times when market requirements are likely to vary, due to new product launches, special promotions, participation in exhibitions, etc.
- Confine your advertising budget to *planned* expenditure. If it is used as a slush fund for things such as plants for the foyer it will be difficult to monitor and administer, and pretty useless when it comes to evaluating results.

- Monitor actual against budgeted expenditure over each period. Be prepared to make adjustments or redistribute resources which you believe could improve your advertising and use your budget effectively. A budget is a way of keeping yourself informed about advertising expenditure; it should never be allowed to decide how it is allocated.
- Create a reserve on which to draw, if necessary, for unexpected or unpredicted events, such as new sales opportunities or market changes which may require advertising support.

The media schedule

When a budget has been set the next step is to decide how best to use it. You may already have ideas about this, but it is necessary to decide which medium, or media, will be used to implement your advertising plan. Media are dealt with in some detail in later chapters and it could be useful to return to this section after reading them.

In advertising there are two kinds of schedule: the media schedule and the production schedule. The media schedule is a product of the advertising plan and covers all projected advertising (when and where space will be booked, copy dates, origination or production dates, distribution dates for sales letters and direct mail, etc) over a given period, usually a year, though it can be less. In short, the media schedule indicates how you propose to distribute your advertising. A production schedule is exactly what its name implies, and is dealt with in Chapter 11, Origination and Production.

A media schedule is dictated by the market sectors identified and what it costs to use them. There is rarely only one appropriate advertising medium: the prime question is where you can get the best return for the money you plan to spend on advertising, and this could involve research. Individual companies will almost certainly not have all the market research facilities and resources which big agencies use on their clients' behalf, but the alternative isn't to work in the dark and hope for the best.

Assemble as much factual information as you can lay your hands on, and keep the advertising budget handy too – it might need adjusting to reflect your anticipated expenditure more accurately after the media schedule has been decided. At this stage a draft media schedule will show whether any budgetary changes are necessary or desirable.

Rate cards (see pp 23–5), statistical information, sales forecasts and projected product changes and developments are relevant, as is penetration (see pp 25 and 29). For press advertising, calculations can be based on a 'cost per thousand' (see p 27) and for other media, such as sales letters and direct mail, a 'cost per enquiry' or 'cost per sale'; all help to make the media schedule realistic.

The time-scale of the schedule is also important. This should be determined by the speed at which the results from your advertising can be expected and quantified: this is the only reliable test of whether a media schedule is matched to your advertising intentions (see Chapter 13, Testing). If, over relatively short periods, results can be evaluated with some accuracy it could be better to have a short-term media schedule, or to review the schedule fairly frequently and adjust it to reflect penetration, though any alternative media then considered must be investigated, and care taken to avoid penalties for short-notice cancellations (see p 35).

The more reliable your market information the more effective the media schedule will be in helping to carry out your advertising intentions: advertising is market-led; but markets can change for a variety of reasons. Technological, social and economic developments, as well as fads and fashions, may shift the marketing goal-posts.

For example, when all computers were large, expensive, complicated machines and used mainly for specialised applications, their market sectors were comparatively well defined. When smaller, cheaper computers were developed for personal, leisure, educational and business uses, the computer industry was forced to change its advertising to meet the needs, expectations and applications of new markets.

Media themselves also change: new journals are launched and existing ones wax and wane; space costs do not remain fixed for long.

Thus a workable plan, and its dependent media schedule, isn't what you would *like* to happen, but what, within your resources, you believe you *can* accomplish. I'm afraid that means more questions which only you can answer, the most difficult being 'What *identifiable* needs, interests and expectations do the customers and potential customers in your market sectors have in common?'

Factors such as income, age, social and financial status, sex and geographical location may have to be taken into account (see pp 27–8). Some can be ascertained fairly easily; others can only be determined through research which, if you don't conduct it yourself, can be expensive . . . and doesn't always come up with the right answers.

Specialised or high-value products are advertised where people who need, or can afford, them are likely to notice them; less specialised, or more accessible, products and services can be advertised wherever they are likely to attract the attention of anyone who can be convinced they are worth having. In the latter case a 'media spread' may be necessary, whereas in the former the right medium, or media, could be well defined, the only question being how effective the advertisements are.

Action guide

- Read media selection, pp 21–32, first.
- Select the media best suited to your advertising strategy.
- Decide over what period the media schedule should run.
- Estimate how any anticipated changes in products (such as a product launch) or trading condition (such as participation in an exhibition) could possibly influence the advertising schedule during its projected period.
- Decide what benefits or advantages should be highlighted in your advertising.
- Evaluate any additional or supporting media worth your consideration.

CHAPTER 2
Press Advertising

The medium in which an advertisement is placed has a direct bearing on the stages through which it passes up to, and even beyond, its appearance. I will deal first with press (publications) advertising since this is used extensively – sometimes exclusively – by most advertisers.

Newspaper and periodical advertising is relatively easy to use: the advertiser books specified spaces for specific insertions and prepares advertisements in accordance with the media schedule and the production requirements of the publication. The press is, in effect, an advertising bazaar where complete advertising packages can be bought; but remember, what you are buying is advertising *space*, not advertisements. An ineffectual ad remains ineffectual, and an ad in the wrong place, or at the wrong time, will not produce the anticipated response. (This is a caution against believing that media selection is the beginning and end of press advertising!)

Media selection and analysis

Media selection obviously precedes the preparation of a media schedule, which is why I suggested, under this heading in Chapter 1, that further investigation could be necessary before embarking on it.

Your own knowledge and experience count for a lot because unbiased guidance is hard to find in this area, because newspapers and magazines are competitive, and whatever else they offer an advertiser they are unlikely to turn down business.

If you don't already know in which newspapers or journals your advertising will stand the best chance of being effective there is only one thing to do: find out as much as you can about *all* the likely ones – it is common sense to get to know as much as possible about what is on offer before deciding how and where to spend your money. Media selection for some products and services can be relatively straightforward. For others, especially consumer products in wider, less precisely defined or more geographically dispersed markets, thorough *media analysis* will be necessary.

The most valuable reference source for this is BRAD *(British Rate and Data)*, updated and published monthly by Maclean Hunter Ltd, Chalk Lane, Cockfosters Road, Barnet, Hertfordshire EN4 0BU.

For practical purposes, newspapers and periodicals can be classified as follows. The figures indicate the approximate

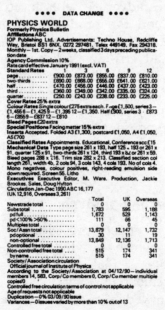

Figure 2.1 *A sample listing from* BRAD

Reproduced by kind permission of Maclean Hunter Limited

number of separate listings in BRAD for each category but, with new titles and some closures, they vary:

Newspapers: National dailies (12)
National Sundays (12)
Regional dailies (mornings and evenings) (121)
Regional Sundays (16)
Weeklies (1155)
Free newspapers (freesheets) (1157)
Foreign language dailies (4)
Sporting dailies (2)

Periodicals: Consumer (general interest, including women's and special interest publications such as hobbies and sporting activities) (2169)
Business publications including trade and technical magazines, newsletters and journals produced for particular organisations, such as chambers of commerce (4263).

The complete list, including a few other categories, numbers around 9012 publications.

First identify *all* the publications which are likely to cover your target readership (existing and potential customers). Perhaps you already know them, but check with BRAD anyway. The list could be long or short, depending on the size and nature of the perceived market. At this stage, do not exclude titles which may not yet have been decided upon: though your budget will be a powerful deciding factor in media selection, you still have a choice, so do not restrict your options. In some cases, eg when the target readership cannot be reached by one or two publications, you may need a 'spread' of advertising, and media analysis can sometimes suggest a better way of spending your money.

How to handle press advertising

When a shortlist of publications has been made, advertising rate cards should be obtained from their respective advertising departments. *Rate cards* differ in the amount of information they contain, but usually show circulation figures, publication frequency, advertising production deadlines and technical requirements, space rates and maybe a breakdown of readership into specified categories. Some rate cards show 'standard' rates, together with rates for such things as particular positions or colour, and discounts for such things as 'block' bookings. Rates for advertising inserts (see p 34), if accepted, will also be shown. Some publications provide quite hefty packages of statistical and analytical data with their rate cards and most of them follow up enquiries with a sales call from an advertising rep.

Whether you meet advertising representatives personally is for you to decide, though once advertising has been placed it is important for whoever manages it to have direct access to someone who can give information and, if required, advice and guidance on practical and technical matters.

Before booking an ad it is essential to establish with the publication concerned *exactly* what you will be getting for what you pay: there should be no unspecified extras, eg for special positions or 'bleed' (see p 105). Also, published rates notwithstanding, the media compete for your advertising and there could be occasions when discounts will be negotiable, so don't be in too much of a hurry to sign the contract!

The principal cost of press advertising is related mainly to *circulation* – the number of copies printed or distributed – but also to *penetration*, the extent to which a publication can be shown to reach its defined readership.

Circulation figures alone don't offer much information about how the readers of a publication react to its editorial and advertising contents. To assess whether the circulation is likely to contain a larger or smaller proportion of the target readership for your advertising needs deeper digging. If you are not familiar with a newspaper or publication under consideration examine a few issues closely and try to assess whether, in appearance, editorial and advertising content, it is likely to reach your target readership. If you think so there are some more things you will want to find out.

RATES & DATA

SIZE	MONOCHROME	FULL COLOUR	TYPE AREA Depth x Width (mm)
Double Page Spread	£900	£1750	267 x 380
Whole Page	£475	£925	267 x 190
Cover Position	–	£1050	267 x 190
Half Page Horizontal	£260	£520	130 x 190
Half Page Vertical	£260	£520	267 x 93
Quarter Page	£167	£275	130 x 93
Eighth Page	£100	–	63 x 93

Inserts accepted by arrangement
CLASSIFIED ADVERTISEMENTS
(All classified advertisements must be prepaid)
Private Classified 45p per word (Minimum 15 words)
Semi Display – £8.50 per s.c.c.
Trade Directory (3cm x 1 col.) – £150 (1or 12 months)

MECHANICAL DATA

Finished Size A4. Printed sheet fed litho
Screen: (Mono) 120 line screen (Colour) 133 line screen
Camera Ready Artwork or Film Positives
Trimmed Size 297mm x 210mm Bleed Size 303mm x 216mm
DPS 297mm x 420mm
No essential matter to appear within 12mm of any trimmed edge. Typesetting, Photography, Artwork and Colour Separations, where necessary, will be charged extra at cost; rates quoted above are for insertion only. Proofs will be supplied only upon specific request, for correction and return within 48 hours of receipt.

PUBLICATION AND COPY DATES
Monthly

Each issue on sale last week of month preceding cover date. Copy for typesetting required seven weeks before publication. Artwork required five weeks before publication.

Figure 2.2 *A sample rate card*

Reproduced by kind permission of *Military Illustrated*

Types of circulation

There are two types of circulation, paid and controlled. A paid circulation at least shows that advertising is received by readers who are prepared to pay for the journal because they want it. Increasingly, however, many business, and some consumer, magazines have controlled circulations (cc), which means they are distributed, usually to registered readers, free of charge. These publications rely for their profitability entirely on advertising revenue. If they are well produced, with good editorial and advertising content, cc journals may be considered alongside paid circulation magazines, especially if they reach a precisely targeted readership though, in the case of cc journals, a 'guaranteed circulation' does not add up to the same thing as a paid readership.

Circulations are monitored by the Audit Bureau of Circulations which issues an ABC figure based on the certified number of copies of a dated issue sold or distributed excluding, in the case of publications with a cover price, voucher (free) copies. ABC figures are usually published by magazines and if available they are always given in BRAD.

Readerships

A useful distinction can be made between 'vertical' and 'horizontal' readerships. The former indicates that the majority of readers are interested in well-defined, often specialised, subjects, eg fishing, computers, cookery or a particular industry or profession. Many cc journals have vertical readerships. A horizontal, or general, readership covers more diverse reader categories in terms of personal interests, and maybe of age, sex, occupation, income, social grading, geographical distribution or politics. Horizontal publications may have larger circulations than vertical ones, and the cost of advertising in them will then reflect this wider appeal. A crude distinction between horizontal and vertical readerships is insufficient for detailed media analysis, but a useful reminder of primary differences.

It is naturally easier to identify a target readership in vertical publications than in horizontal ones. If a product is likely to interest, say, only dentists, an advertisement in a journal which most dentists are likely to read professionally will reach your target readership: in this case it doesn't matter whether the reader is old or young, male or female, married or single, or what his or her hobbies may be provided he or she is a dentist, and the choice of this publication could involve no more than an assessment of its penetration.

For example, free weekly newspapers (freesheets) are by definition both horizontal and cc. Their increase in number – about 1157 compared with about 1155 regional weekly newspapers with paid circulations in 1991 – suggests that many of them are now carrying a sufficient amount of advertising to justify their production and distribution costs.

Some important terms

For sound media analysis a working knowledge of some periodical publishing terms is necessary. These include:

Average issue readership
This is an estimate of the number of people who read the average issue of a newspaper or magazine, based on the number who have read or looked at its most recent issue for at least two minutes – hard to establish with accuracy, but it can be a salutary reminder of how little reader-time the advertiser buys!

Cost per thousand (CPT)
The average cost to the advertiser of 1000 exposures of an advertisement to a target readership is a rough and ready way of making a cost comparison between publications, but remember that it does not give any indication of such things as readership quality and response rate. The calculation is made by dividing the cost per page by the publication's certified circulation, so if the cost per page is £500 and the circulation is 100,000, the CPT is £5.

Demographic analysis
This is the analysis of readerships or audiences by age, sex or

social class. Demographic analysis is widely used by advertising agencies and depends for its accuracy on statistical data which must be regularly updated and expertly interpreted. Demographic analysis helps to identify a target readership or audience. Social grading is one demographic classification often used in advertising and the media. This is based on the occupations (or, if retired, former occupations) of the main providers in households. The recognised gradings are:

A   (upper middle class): higher managerial; administrative or professional

B   (middle class): intermediate managerial; administrative or professional

C1   (lower middle class): supervisory or clerical, junior managerial; administrative or professional

C2   (skilled working class): skilled manual workers

D   (working class): semi-skilled and unskilled manual workers

E   (people at the lowest level of subsistence): state pensioners living entirely on their pensions, casual workers, the unemployed, the lowest grade workers.

Whatever personal reservations one might have about these gradings, they at least help to identify the assumed spending potential in each classification, and can lead to other useful deductions. For example, one might expect to find proportionately more mothers and fathers maintaining young children among class C1 than class E readers and fewer car owners in class D than in class A. Anyway, that's the code!

Coverage
Coverage is not the same as circulation. The fact that a magazine is bought or distributed does not guarantee that it will be read by everyone who gets it. Coverage analysis seeks to establish the number of people in a target readership/ audience who have taken at least one opportunity of seeing an advertisement. Some publications offer their own coverage analysis; others don't. It is virtually impossible for an advertiser to obtain really reliable and exact information on coverage.

Duplication
Duplication is the number of people likely to read more than one publication in a specified field. For example, at the moment printers have a choice of at least five trade journals, all cc. There is therefore a strong possibility of duplication. On the other hand, fossil collectors are (so far as I am aware) catered for specifically in only one journal, and there is little likelihood of duplication.

Universe
This is the total number of members in a target audience, ie the maximum potential audience for a targeted advertisement. It is used more in TV than in press advertising.

Reader penetration
Reader penetration is the number of people likely to see the advertisements in a publication of a given circulation and frequency. For example, daily newspapers are read more or less immediately they are published and discarded soon afterwards, though they may well be read by more than one person. Weekly and monthly consumer magazines have a potentially higher penetration, since they are likely to be kept for longer periods and seen by more than one reader. Publication frequency is an aspect of reader penetration, though repetition – the number of *individual* exposures of an ad – must also be considered: daily and weekly newspapers are able to repeat and reinforce an advertising message more often, and with greater topicality, than journals with longer intervals between publication.

Position
The placing, or positioning, of an ad within a publication is important in terms of its visibility. Readers do not normally buy newspapers and magazines only to read the advertisements (though, occasionally, they may do). Bearing this in mind, and the time – maybe only a few seconds – which an advertisement has to capture a reader's interest and convey its message, the position an ad occupies in a publication can have a considerable effect on its visibility and response rate. Size and colour are also visibility factors, but advertisements

appear together with news, features and other advertisements, all of which compete for the reader's attention.
However attractive and persuasive an ad may be, it cannot
produce results until it has been noticed and read.

Page traffic
Page traffic is the frequency with which the pages of a
publication are likely to be scanned by its readers. For
example, in TV programme magazines advertisers are particularly concerned with page traffic. These magazines print a
week's programme information day by day so readers are
considered less likely to 'flip' backwards or forwards through
the pages. The aim of the advertiser is to be noticed, and
features, competitions, readers' letters and other editorial
items encourage page traffic. *Radio Times* has experimented
with several editorial formats to this end. In newspapers, the
TV and radio programme pages, strip cartoons and other
regular features attract page traffic and encourage advertising
on pages which would otherwise be less popular with
advertisers. The most well-trafficked advertising positions
can usually be identified by their position in the publication,
and how much they cost to book.

In some cases the attractiveness of a straightforward space
booking can be influenced by additional considerations. For
example:

Advertising features

Advertising features seek to attract advertising supported by
editorial text and illustrations. Most newspapers and magazines sell advertising space in special features in which
advertisements are printed in a format similar to the publication's normal editorial content. When offered space in such
features the advertiser should consider carefully how his or
her advertisement could benefit from the formula. The
majority of readers are well able to distinguish between
independent editorial and advertising, so features should be
judged strictly on the interest that readers are likely to show in
the information they contain: after all, you can never force

anybody to read something which doesn't capture and hold their attention.

Effective though 'editorial format' can appear to be to advertisers it is, to my mind, sometimes in danger of looking like a confidence trick. Credibility is important in advertising, and anything which detracts from it should be avoided.

If advertising features are well targeted and well written they can attract considerable reader-attention. For example, the special features published by the *Financial Times* are often of high quality and interest, and consequently give high visibility to the advertising associated with them.

Newspapers and magazines advise potential advertisers in advertising features to plan well in advance. Space rates may be lower than normal for the publication.

A decision about whether to participate in an advertising feature should be a calculated one, and take account of the company's advertising budget and advertising strategy as a whole. It may also be prudent to ascertain what other ads will be appearing in the same feature. If such features amount to little more than thinly disguised, slackly written puffs for advertisers they are not only time and money wasters, but may also damage the credibility of the advertiser.

Advertorials

'Advertorial' is a mongrel word, and a mongrel concept. It suggests that advertisements in a newspaper or magazine which are designed and presented to look like that publication's normal editorial are likely to receive closer attention from readers than straightforward advertising. Some publications will not accept advertorials; others encourage them.

In my view advertorials are based on two questionable premises: one is that readers cannot recognise paid advertising when they see it if it is presented in the same typographical style as that used for news and features, and second that advertisers are naïve enough to believe this!

The difference between advertorials and advertising features (see p 30) appears slight, but it is important: advertising features are intended to attract readers' attention and stimulate their interest in particular products or subjects; but the editorial part of an advertising feature cannot itself be purchased by an advertiser; it is there to reinforce or support the accompanying advertising.

The advertiser might be induced to use advertorials in the belief that, due to their editorial format, they are more believable, or offer an opportunity for writing longer, more persuasive, more fully explanatory copy; but advertorials transgress a basic tenet of all good advertising: that the reader should not be made to feel that he or she has been tricked in this case into believing that an advertisement is anything other than an advertisement.

The same applies to advertisements which are typographically designed and laid out to look like editorial, whether or not they are headed (as they should be) 'advertisement' or 'advertiser's announcement'.

Classified advertisements

Classified advertisements are sometimes neglected by advertisers – and, indeed, in books about advertising – but there can be good reasons for using them. Classified ads appear on certain fixed and classified pages separate from the main editorial and advertising contents of a publication. They may be 'semi-display' (ie printed in accordance with the design and copy supplied by the advertiser or an advertising agency) or printed in a standard format decided by the publication. Recruitment advertising (see Chapter 8) is often semi-displayed. If classified ads are needed for any purpose they should be part of both the media schedule (see pp 18–20) and the production schedule (see pp 114–16), when classified advertising should receive as much careful attention as you would give to display advertising. Relatively low cost has nothing to do with it: a classified ad must be made to work just as hard as a displayed ad – maybe even harder, because classifieds appear on pages which contain other ads in the same classification, and all are competing for reader attention.

Figure 2.3 *A classified advertisement*

Reproduced by kind permission of ATA West Advertising

Semi-display classified advertising should aim to provide as much factual information as possible in the space available, but every effort must be made to make the ad distinctive and easy to assimilate. Classified pages are 'busy' and are read quickly. Readers are easily distracted by their sheer volume of advertising. Making optimum use of the available space calls for copy which has been carefully written and ruthlessly stripped of inessentials. Think of your classified advertising as you would if you were trying to gain somebody's undivided interest and attention in a noisy, crowded room!

Design your classifieds for quick, effortless reading. Excessively small type and mixtures of many different typefaces and sizes should both be avoided. People tend to read classifieds selectively, and mainly for factual information. Make sure that they can find what they're looking for easily, and know where to get it. (See copywriting, pp 86–9 and design and layouts, pp 90–94.)

If classified advertising is used regularly there is much to be said for devising and maintaining a consistent, identifiable typographical style and layout, and maybe a company logo, which will allow your ads a measure of individuality.

Classifieds are sometimes used to draw the reader's attention to displayed advertising in another part of the same publication. This is not a common practice, but one I believe worth considering.

Loose inserts

Most magazines will accept pre-printed inserts. Their advantage, compared with bound-in displayed ads, is that, being produced separately and independently, they can be designed more freely and are subject to fewer technical constraints.

When a magazine publisher, I was occasionally told by readers that they found advertising inserts a nuisance. All the same, the number of inserts we carried, and the money and effort put into their production by advertisers and agencies, suggested that this form of advertising was considered cost-effective for certain products and purposes.

Inserts in magazines are also an easy way of distributing printed advertising to a defined readership. For such purposes inserts can be regarded as a form of direct mail since they can be used to distribute items such as price-lists or information which is not likely to be available in a company's other advertising.

Rates for pre-printed inserts are given in the rate cards of publications which accept them.

Now for some practicalities which every advertiser needs to know:

Copy dates

It is essential for press advertising to be supplied to the publication in which it will appear by a copy deadline (copy date). The publication will not accept responsibility for advertisements which miss their copy dates, so copy dates are important. They differ from one publication to another, and will also depend on whether the ad is single or multi-colour, pre-printed, printed as part of the normal printing run (run of press) or has to be printed separately.

Copy dates for national dailies are usually between three and five days for black-and-white ads, between five and six weeks for pre-printed colour and between four and ten days for run-of-press colour. They are longer for weekly and monthly magazines. The rate card, or the publication's advertising department, will advise on copy dates.

Cancellations

If an advertiser wishes to cancel an ad after it has been booked the advertising department of the newspaper or magazine must be notified immediately. If this is not done within a stated period the advertiser may be required to pay for the space. In some cases colour advertising already booked may not be cancelled at all without incurring a penalty.

Cancellation periods should be noted when space is booked. The period for cancellation without penalty depends on the position and size of advertisement(s) and ranges from 4 to 28 days for black-and-white ads in national daily news-papers (up to 90 days for colour) and from 6 to 12 weeks for general interest magazines (12 to 16 weeks for colour).

Mechanical requirements

Most publications publish their mechanical (technical) requirements in their rate cards and can readily explain what they are. As well as ensuring that an ad fits the space booked for it, the advertiser may also need to take into account the printing process used to produce the magazine, especially if colour will be used. Much depends on how and where the ad is originated, but if it is originated by the advertiser as camera-ready copy (see pp 101–2) or artwork (see pp 104–7) technical requirements can be quite complex.

Action guide

- Never handle press advertising routinely. Analyse and evaluate media before using your budget. Be prepared to redistribute your budget and amend your media schedule, if necessary, to take account of special rates, discounts or a change in your advertising strategy.
- Keep all contracts and a record of all space bookings and cancellation periods. Take careful note of copy dates and mechanical requirements.
- File useful data, such as rate cards and media analysis, for future reference and use all the believable and relevant statistical and marketing information you can acquire to assist you in making an intelligent and informed media selection.
- Be prepared to adapt your space buying to unexpected changes in your market or trading conditions.
- Annuals, year-books and directories with extended or irregular frequencies may be considered part of space advertising. If they are, personal knowledge of the readership and penetration of the publication is probably the most reliable guide to whether advertising in a particular publication could be of benefit. For example, products and services which rely heavily on telephone enquiries may use displayed advertising in classified telephone directories, or a company which serves a particular trade or profession will take space in year-books and other reference books regularly used by members of that trade or profession.

- Make classified advertising part of your schedule if it is used (eg for attracting new staff, see Chapter 8, Recruitment Advertising); it warrants attention. Classified ads (see pp 33–6) can also be used to reinforce or draw attention to displayed advertising.

In terms of cost per exposure the press is a relatively cheap and easy-to-manage advertising medium. The advertiser can calculate on a cost-per-reader basis. The advertising departments of newspapers and magazines are usually willing to offer advice and guidance if asked.

I have dealt in some detail with press advertising, but this could be the right place to say that it is not always wise to put all one's eggs into one advertising basket, however capacious and accommodating that basket appears. A media 'spread' is sometimes desirable – even essential – for advertising certain products and services. Other media, such as sales letters, direct mail and point-of-sale displays, are discussed in this book, and any reader who is unfamiliar with them should at least make their acquaintance before committing too high a proportion of his or her budget to press advertising.

CHAPTER 3
Direct Mail

Direct mail (sometimes called *direct response*) includes all postal advertising used to sell or promote products and services, produce sales leads and distribute advertising material, even if no purchase is involved. Direct response includes press and broadcast advertising where an individual response is invited. I shall omit product selling through press advertisements (sometimes called *off-the-page selling*), unaddressed items such as free newspapers, coupons and mail order catalogues, since these are all more or less specialised operations.

Direct mail using the UK postal services doubled between 1983 and 1990 to more than two billion items a year, an estimated 32 items per head of the population, split approximately 50/50 between consumer products and business services and supplies.

Direct mail is used by a wide variety of advertisers, and has proved successful in selling specialised, as well as consumer, products and services.

It is as well to come to grips straight away with its 'junk-mail' image: some people ignore, or resent, this form of advertising, which means that they will be considerably less responsive than others to direct mail. The medium has gone some way towards changing any junk-mail image it may have acquired, largely through self-regulation and the statutory protection now given against fraudulent or otherwise unsatisfactory trading.

It is above all a competitive medium, the pace being set by regular users such as book clubs, banks, insurance companies and building societies, though this need not mean that only the most well-heeled and ambitious advertiser can make use of it. Outside creative and production services will almost certainly be needed for a fully fledged direct mail campaign, and these are not cheap. Properly handled, direct mail has certain advantages over other media – mainly controllability and accountability. Direct mail packages can be 'tailored' to products and services, and aimed with precision at target markets. It can also be a somewhat wasteful medium if not used expertly. Success is measured strictly by response: a mail shot is *seen* to work . . . or not, as the case may be!

Well-honed techniques have evolved in virtually all the areas where direct mail is used effectively, and much can be learned from other practitioners. High-grade technical guidance and information, some of it free of charge, is available from the sources listed at the end of this chapter. Anything which identifies potential customers, or indicates where they can be reached, improves the chance of success. Direct mail should not be a shot in the dark, and time spent on planning and research will be rewarded.

Planning direct mail

Here is an outline plan for a direct mail shot:

1. Define its purpose.
2. Identify the target sector of the market.
3. Produce or obtain a mailing list appropriate to that sector (see Chapter 5, Mailing Lists).
4. Draft copy and layout for the package, including the envelope.
5. Estimate creative, production and distribution costs to establish realistic total cost for the package. Check against budget.
6. Produce finished copy and artwork.

7. Initiate production by producing specifications, obtaining estimates for production and distribution, and preparing (see Chapter 5, Mailing Lists).
8. Produce the package.
9. Make sure that you have everything you need to handle response promptly and efficiently.
10. Mail the package.
11. Analyse response. Does it come up to your expectations? What can you learn which could improve your next package?
12. Check returned mail and amend the mailing list if any item has been incorrectly addressed.

Targeting

Match the package to the known, or perceived, interests, preoccupations and activities of the kind of person you want to respond: target it to a customer profile, not a vague 'customer concept'. Try to visualise the *sort* of person who will receive the package and the environment in which it will be examined. Is the reader young or old? Male or female? Is he or she at home or at work? In what kind of home or what sort of workplace? How much, if anything, is he or she likely to know already about your company and what is being offered? The better you understand the intended recipient the more detailed will be your reader profile. Never mind how clever *you* think your package is, keep the reader in focus all the time.

The uses of direct mail are so diverse that a standard guide on how to design and produce a package is impossible. It may contain anything from a single letter to as many as nine or ten printed items, but one thing is certain: the package must be gauged to the recipient's, not the advertiser's, expectations. Distribution lists, customer profiles, geographic and demographic information, the production schedule and the size of the mailing – all, to a greater or lesser extent – influence the design, content and presentation of a direct mail shot. The only consistent requirement is that it must provide some means by which the recipient can respond and obtain whatever is being offered.

Direct mail can often be used on a smaller and more selective scale for sales letters (see Chapter 4), customer communications, to distribute items such as brochures or to stimulate enquiries or sales leads. Whatever the reason is for using it, take it seriously: casual direct mail is a complete waste of advertising effort and money. Brief copywriters and designers clearly and fully: make sure that they know what's expected and when it is expected. Copywriters and illustrators should be in possession of all information and research which will help them to understand the purpose of the mail shot and its targeted market.

The package

Copywriting for direct mail shares many of the conditions outlined for sales letters (Chapter 4) and copywriting generally, but differs in some important respects from displayed advertising. Obviously, direct mail is personally addressed so, aside from overt personalisation (see pp 49–50), it must engage the reader at a personal level. Assuming a short attention span, short copy would appear to be the watchword. Yet the package must convey not only what is offered, but do so fully and persuasively, and indicate exactly what action you wish the recipient to take. Long letters may well be read more attentively by people who do not receive a large quantity of personal mail than by those who receive mainly business correspondence.

Try out original ideas, but do not strive after effect. Recently, I received a plain, hand-addressed envelope containing a badly creased sales letter. Smoothing it out I read that the sender had 'pre-crumpled' it ready for throwing away because 'people like you don't take any notice of direct mail'; I read the letter! Only results or test mailings can prove whether such unorthodox approaches are more effective than conventional packages.

Help the Aged

THE TIME TO CARE IS NOW

St. James's Walk London EC1R 0BE
Telephone: 071-253 0253
Patron: HRH The Princess of Wales

January, 1991

****
      With this letter I've enclosed a 4" plastic square.
      Now hold it up to one eye and try to look through it.
****

Dear Friend

      How much were you able to see?

      Not much, not even your own hands in front of your face. Or the
ground you are standing on.

      And if you tried to walk even a few steps you'd almost certainly
stumble.

      This is what it's like to be blinded by cataracts.

      And it's why I'm writing to ask you to help us by
sending a donation today.

      As you've seen, in the safety of your own home, trying to cope
without good eyesight would be hard enough.

      For poor, elderly people overseas it is far, far worse.

      Imagine what it's like for an elderly person in India or Africa
trying to buy the food they need in a crowded market, then walking
home five or six miles over rough terrain and narrow paths. Or
looking after tiny children in a smoky hut with an open fire on the
floor.

      The fact is that for elderly men and women overseas, losing their

Please read on ...

Figure 3.1 *A direct mail letter. Its envelope is on page 47*

Page Two

eyesight is one of the worst things that can possibly happen.

Let me give you just one example, from the many many, sad and needy cases we know of in India alone. 50 year old Rati Ram was already blind in his left eye when further tragedy struck : his wife Shangani died, leaving him to look after his nine year old son alone.

This already difficult situation turned to disaster when a cataract began to cloud the vision in his right eye. Before long he was totally blind. Rati Ram now relied on his son for everything. The future they faced together was unimaginably bleak.

To see once-proud men and women being led by little children because they can't even walk a few paces in safety is one of the most moving sights I've witnessed.

That's why Help the Aged is so determined to carry on the fight against crippling eye diseases. And why it's so important you join in this effort today.

HOW YOU CAN MAKE A BLIND PERSON SEE AGAIN

There are many causes of loss of eyesight in Africa, Asia and Latin America - but just three main ones: cataracts (gradual milky clouding of the eyes); and two serious eye diseases - glaucoma (swollen eyeballs) and trachoma, where due to repeated infection and scarring the upper eyelid turns inwards so the lashes scrape and scratch the surface of the eye. Every blink is agony.

Right this minute, as you read this letter, elderly people are suffering in pain or they are gradually going blind.

But the worst of this tragedy is that it needn't happen at all.

You can stop it happening to one person with a gift of just £12.

WHAT YOUR HELP WILL MEAN

With modern surgical techniques cataract operations are simple and quick. It takes a specially trained surgical team less than half an hour to remove the cataract. In just one week the bandages can usually come off. With special spectacles, and a little after care, it's not long before the patient can see again properly.

Page Three

For elderly people who have all but given up on life it's more
than a miracle. The look on their faces when they see their loved
ones again is more wonderful than I can possibly describe - and I've
seen it many, many times.

Most clearly of all I remember an elderly woman living in a
village outside Delhi. One thought filled her day above all others
- the approaching birth of her first grandchild.

But tragedy was looming. Cataracts were fast clouding her vision
in both eyes. As each day went by, her sight got worse and worse.
Finally her last great hope was dashed : she lost her sight
altogether.

Then her family heard of the mobile eye clinic supported by Help
the Aged. Despite many anxieties, she agreed to attend, and was
operated on immediately.

Just 40 days later the doctors took off her bandages. You can
imagine her feelings as she saw her tiny grandchild for the very first
time. She picked him up and simply wept for joy.

NOW PLAY YOUR PART

A cataract operation costs just £12 in countries like India and
Africa. Most eye units are staffed with doctors, some trained by Help
the Aged, who gladly give their skills and time free of charge to help
those in need.

But they lack the money to buy anaesthetics, surgical
instruments, medicines, bandages for after-care and, of course, the
spectacles.

Now you can play your part in the miracle of restoring eyesight
by helping to provide these things.

And the cure for painful trachoma is even simpler. Often a
little anti-biotic ointment is all it takes. And even advanced cases
only need minor surgery to ease the eyelashes back to their proper
position.

The ointment costs 10p a tube. The operation no more than £12.

Please read on ...

Page Four

These small amounts are all that come between tragic blindness, and being able to see properly again. But unless you help us, the suffering will go on.

Help the Aged is often the only source of hope for poor, elderly people overseas. Please, I ask you, find it in your heart to give the priceless gift of sight.

Of all the requests that will be made of you this year to help those in need, please make this a priority if you possibly can.

I can guarantee that the money you send will go straight to helping elderly people overseas who need it most.

Please send a donation of whatever amount you can spare. And if you can help two or more people to see again, that would be magnificent.

And do send your gift today. You'll be bringing the day closer when many more impoverished elderly people will shout for joy and say "I can see, I can see again".

With heartfelt thanks for your gift of sight.

Yours sincerely,

Christopher Beer

Dr Christopher Beer
Overseas Director

PS   After the "eye test" I asked you to do at the beginning of this letter you were able to see properly again, just by taking the piece of plastic away from your eyes. A gift of just £12 from you today will do even more for an elderly cataract sufferer overseas. And you'll have given the most valuable gift of all – the priceless gift of sight.

L217

If undelivered please return to:
P.O. Box 464 London EC1B 1BD

♻ Recycled paper

You have this gift... Could you give it to others?

Help the Aged

Reproduced by kind permission of Help the Aged

List, and arrange in order of importance, the benefits/ advantages of your offer and present them in a logical sequence. A direct mail letter should engage the reader's attention quickly and positively and hold it to the end, 'tracking' from one point to the next. Typography, layout and artwork should support and enhance the copy.

Design direct mail packages economically; one good letter is preferable to a confusing assortment of items. Undue elaboration increases production costs without good reason. If you use personalisation (see p 49) design the package for personalisation from the outset and ensure that this can be done as *you* want it done. Match personalised data to the character and typestyle of the text into which it will be incorporated.

When drafting a package, make sure that you are not 'designing in' difficulties or unanticipated costs which could

Please help us keep our mailing list up to date

Tick appropriate box

☐ Please add my name to your mailing list

☐ Please amend my name and address as shown below

☐ Please delete my name from your mailing list

NAME...

POSITION...

ORGANISATION...................................

ADDRESS..

............................POSTCODE..................

TELEPHONE NUMBER.........................

Please keep me informed about new titles on the subjects ticked:

☐ Business and Management   ☐ Transport

☐ Sales and Marketing   ☐ Logistics and Distribution

☐ Finance and Accountancy   ☐ Personal Finance

☐ Small Business   ☐ Careers

☐ Human Resource Management   ☐ Education

☐ Training   ☐ Information Science

Please return the whole envelope, post free, to: FREEPOST 1, Kogan Page, 120 Pentonville Road, London N1 9BR.

Figure 3.2 *A Freepost panel on the back of a direct mail envelope helps to keep your list up to date. The disadvantage of this one is that the Post Office returns 'gone-aways' to the Freepost address, and each one is charged for.*

emerge at the production or distribution stages. Extra operations such as perforating, gumming, laminating and trimming can be expensive. Resist over-elaboration: know what's there and why it's there.

Do not try to achieve too much in a single mailing. As with all advertising, reinforcement and repetition increase the chances of success. A follow-up mailing is often advisable, and should be planned at the same time as the main shot, but repeated identical mailings should be avoided.

Personalisation

Personalisation involves the insertion of variable data, such as names and addresses, during production and is often considered an important element in a direct mail package. The reason is obvious: people take more notice when addressed by name. Every mail shot is personalised to the extent that it is addressed to someone, but full personalisation involves inserting personal names elsewhere than in the address. The frequent use of personalisation for consumer mailings has, to some extent, neutralised its effectiveness: most people are well able to distinguish between a truly personal letter and an item of direct mail.

It is practically impossible to personalise a large mailing without a computerised listing. Computers can easily insert variable data into a printed page: how the technology works is less important than the fact that, if required, it can be done. The real question, from the direct mail user's standpoint, is whether it is necessary and, if so, how to go about it. Using a computerised mailing list, the cost of personalisation will depend on the number, and positions, of the variables inserted, and the size of the mailing.

Plan personalisation in close liaison with production so that the distribution list is available in a form compatible with the equipment and computer program needed to print it. Without early liaison, data-processing problems can arise which make personalisation difficult, or impossible.

Full personalisation requires accurate, well-cleaned and up-to-date lists. If the distribution list is poorly maintained there will be wasted mailings and a reduced response.

Production

All external services needed for production and distribution should be co-ordinated by the advertiser. It is important to know when each stage will be initiated and completed in accordance with a schedule for every mailing.

How a direct mail package is produced depends, of course, on what it contains. Direct mail production houses have equipment and machinery which allow a wide choice of sizes and formats, and facilities for printing, personalisation, folding, inserting, glueing and other operations, to be carried out in-line. Elaborately designed packages will almost certainly require such facilities, and it is as well to be conscious of exceptional production requirements at the design stage.

Distribution and fulfilment

Whether to mail internally or use outside services will again depend on the size of the mailing and the in-house resources available. Large-scale mailings can be addressed, enclosed and distributed rapidly by specialised mailing houses, list brokers and some printers. Lists are valuable and should be protected.

Mailing costs can be reduced substantially if packages are designed and produced in accordance with the Post Office regulations and requirements for bulk mailings. The Post Office also operates Business Reply, Freepost and Admail services which simplify fulfilment. Brochures and information are available from Area Offices. For large mailings a dummy package can be weighed, together with its envelope or cover, to estimate postal costs.

Small test mailings can provide valuable information on how effective a direct mail package is likely to be. If you make test mailings learn everything you can from them, and be ready to change, or even abandon, a mailing if the response to the test package is unsatisfactory.

Action guide

- Cost each mailing fully so that you can judge its result accurately.
- Make a schedule for every mailing from initiation to despatch.
- Observe the laws, regulations and professional standards which apply to direct mail. If in doubt seek advice and guidance from the appropriate organisations (see list at the end of this chapter).
- Mailing lists must be 'clean' and up to date. Regular mailing list maintenance is essential. Whether you buy lists or create your own, make sure that they are up to date (see Chapter 5, Mailing Lists).
- Sequential mailing programmes allow a market to be tackled sector by sector, and packages can be adapted more closely to differing interests and requirements within the target market; but beware of 'overkill'. Cost sequential and follow-up mailings together with the pilot mailing.
- Analyse your direct mail ruthlessly in the light of results. Try to learn something useful from every mailing.
- Study the direct mail packages you see, especially those related to your particular market. Evaluate their concepts and contents, not necessarily to imitate them (though this is not always to be despised!) but mainly to find anything which could be adapted to your requirements.
- Tell recipients exactly what is offered and how to get it, then supply it as promptly and well packaged as you can. Confidence in the value of direct mail on the part of customers is easily shaken by delays in delivery and lack of care after fulfilment.
- Make response easy by using Freepost or reply-paid envelopes. Tell recipients exactly how they should respond.

- Make sure that any commitment on the customer's part is clearly and prominently stated. Offer a money-back guarantee in case of dissatisfaction. If goods are returned on reasonable grounds make refunds quickly and without argument.
- Take care with titles, names and addresses. Check to make certain that all necessary data is available.
- 'Blanket' mailings are wasteful, and rarely effective. Identify your market by sectors, and classify and index your lists. Keep them safe, sorted into target sectors and easily accessible.
- Design the package as a whole, including the envelope and reply coupon or card. Non-standard sizes can be difficult to produce and costly to mail.

Where to get help with direct mail

British Direct Marketing Association
Grosvenor Gardens House
Grosvenor Gardens
London SW1W 0BS
Telephone: 071-630 7322
The BDMA runs workshops on a range of direct marketing topics and offers a legal and commercial advisory service to members.

Direct Mail Producers Association
34 Grand Avenue
London N10 3BP
Telephone: 081-883 9854/5
The DMPA is an association of direct mail agencies and covers the complete range of direct mail services and activities. Its members subscribe to the Code of Advertising Practice, the British Code of Sales Promotion Practice and the Association's own Code of Practice. It will advise on the member agencies best suited to particular needs.

Direct Mail Sales Bureau
14 Floral Street
London WC2E 9RR
Telephone: 071-379 7531
The Bureau is concerned only with consumer direct mail. It can advise on all aspects of a consumer direct mail campaign, and will also buy the necessary services. It can arrange for you to interrogate and use the Consumer Location System.

British List Brokers Association
Springfield House
Princess Street
Bristol BS3 4EF
Telephone: 0272 666900
A professional association of UK list brokers. Contact the BLBA secretary for a full list of members, all of whom comply with the Association's Code of Practice.

Direct Mail Services Standards Board
26 Eccleston Street
London SW1W 9PY
Telephone: 071-824 8651
The DMSSB exists to maintain and enhance professional and ethical standards in direct marketing. The Board will advise advertisers in selecting from among its 155 registered agencies.

Direct Mail Department
The Post Office
Room 195
Post Office Headquarters
33 Grosvenor Place
London SW1X 1PX
Telephone: 071-245 7031
The Post Office has over 200 Postal Sales Representatives in its Area Sales Offices, offering advice and assistance. Phone numbers are in the telephone directory under Post Office Services. The Post Office also publishes a number of useful

guides to direct mail which include details of postal and other services to direct mail advertisers.

Circulars

Leaflets, handbills, samples and similar items circulated directly to households, but not through the regular post, are not, strictly speaking, direct mail advertising, though they can be considered an aspect of it insofar as they reach people directly through the mailbox.

There are, however, several important differences between circulars and direct mail. Obviously, it is impossible to target them, other than geographically or by districts; they are 'blanket' distributions and accurate demographic targeting is not possible. It must also be accepted that many people do not want to receive circulars, and most people take less notice of them than of direct mail. It is also difficult, and sometimes impossible, to measure response. However, this form of advertising is comparatively inexpensive, and can be effective when the advertiser wishes to reach a locally defined market with a specific message.

Distribution can be arranged in several ways. Commercial distribution agencies operate in most areas, using their own delivery personnel. Some offer a 'packaged delivery' comprising several leaflets in a single distribution. The Post Office operates a Household Delivery Service using the normal postal delivery service to distribute leaflets and circulars, details of which can be obtained from the Post Office's local Area Offices listed in the telephone directory.

Most freesheets, and some local newspapers, accept leaflets as inserts, and thus provide a low-cost distribution service within their circulation areas. Local advertising agencies may be able to arrange the distribution of items for their clients. Attempts to distribute leaflets in the streets – eg by tucking them under the wipers of cars – are, in my opinion, wasteful and ineffectual, as well as causing litter.

If this form of advertising is envisaged it will do no harm to check how much of this chapter on direct mail is likely to

Do you need a day nursery for your child?

Hillcroft Nursery School opens on 9 September for children aged 2–5. Supervision by qualified staff. Play and learning. Morning, afternoon or all-day registrations accepted.

For further information or to arrange a visit, please telephone Mrs Jane Robinson on 081-000 0000; 50 Hillcroft Road, Barnlake, NW20.

Figure 3.3 *A handbill*

apply to your ideas about door-to-door distribution. In addition, the advertiser should recognise that leaflets must always be designed to convey their message very quickly, clearly and positively: a large 'package' (in the direct mail sense) is never appropriate. Response to circulars is strictly limited to the number of people who (a) read them, (b) find something of interest or potential value in them, and (c) act on them.

Typical uses for circulars are to promote local services and increase or support sales in shops, restaurants and similar businesses within the distribution area. Because of the ephemeral nature of circulars it is desirable to make quite specific, rather than general, offers. For example, a restaurant could use handbills to promote a special Christmas menu, or a store to offer particular products. In every case it is, of course, essential that the leaflet tells the recipient what's offered and where to get it. One way of monitoring response to circulars is to offer a premium, such as a special price advantage to customers who can produce the advertisement at the point of sale. (See Chapter 9, Premiums and Promotions.)

Circulars for house-to-house distribution are best designed specifically for this purpose. To circulate expensively produced printed literature, such as product catalogues, in this way can be wasteful, though it is sometimes worthwhile using a circular to offer more elaborately designed and produced literature.

Size is important. If you can get everything you need to say on to one side of a single page, do so. Single A4 or A5 pages (handbills) can easily be folded and slipped through letterboxes; a single fold, making a four-page A4 leaflet, should be the maximum size for door-to-door distribution, bearing in mind that if the quantity required for distribution is high, folding and enveloping could be a significant cost. If distribution agencies or newspaper inserts are used it is as well to check whether circulars above a certain size or bulk are acceptable.

Keeping in mind the need to get the message over clearly and quickly, the design and presentation of circulars should be bold and arresting. They must not only claim immediate attention, but also reward it immediately. Crude, poorly designed leaflets stand little chance. Properly used, colour can be an advantage. The circular should aim to convey the nature and quality of the product and service being advertised. Typographical elegance may be appropriate for an antique shop but not for a local garage.

Action guide

- Make production and distribution part of your advertising budget: you should know how much it costs to reach a specified number of households.
- Identify your distribution area, and arrange for distribution *before* you write and design the circular. You can then order the required quantity for printing and avoid waste.
- Examine the circulars you receive at home. Evaluate them in terms of the aforementioned criteria, and don't be afraid to adapt those you consider effective to your particular needs.
- Design and distribute in accordance with the kind of product or service offered, and the kind of people who may be expected to live in the areas where they will be distributed.
- Use large, bold, display typefaces and short copy.
- Tell recipients *exactly* what you are offering and where it can be obtained.
- Offer a price reduction or some other inducement on production of the circular whenever possible to check response.
- A circular in a printed envelope addressed to 'the occupier' is more likely to be examined than an unenclosed circular. It also provides additional space for an advertising message.
- Make use of existing distribution networks such as newspapers whenever possible, or circular distribution agencies which have some knowledge of the localities being circularised.

- Follow-up circulars are rarely necessary: unless you know exactly what the response has been to a circular it is probably a waste of money to try a second or third distribution.

CHAPTER 4
Sales (or Circular) Letters

Sales letters can be regarded as a form of direct mail though they call for separate consideration. Though less complicated and expensive to produce than direct mail packages, they need careful attention and should be treated as part of a company's advertising. If standard sales letters are seen simply as cheap, quick, *ad hoc* communications they risk being ineffectual.

An indication whether a sales letter is likely to serve a useful purpose can be gained by asking what it could achieve over and above existing advertising or sales promotion. Could it tell the recipient more than he or she already knows about the company? Could it, directly or indirectly, stimulate an enquiry? Could it support or reinforce other advertising? Could it help your sales force to operate more effectively in any way?

Here's an example of a well-targeted sales letter. Knowing that environmental issues are now receiving considerable public attention a paper manufacturer sent letters to paper merchants and printers describing the company's investment in pollution control equipment, and listing the recycled papers recently added to its product lines. This information is of interest to those who have to answer customers' questions about the environmental issues related to papermaking. The company also promoted its environmental policy in its published advertising, but decided that the message could be reinforced by writing directly to the people who meet end-users, and need such information at their fingertips.

Sales letters should always be treated as personal communications. If they are not to be treated as circulars they should contain information of direct, and preferably personal, interest to whoever receives them. A sales letter need not invite a buying decision, but it should imply that some action should be taken. Letters can be used to initiate sales leads or to communicate new information, such as a product launch or an improvement in services.

Letters can also be an effective way of maintaining contact with retail outlets, branches, agencies or dealers. They should be regarded as sales letters since they are addressed to the people who can influence sales and are in direct contact with customers. Information on price changes, products, services, promotions and, indeed, anything which helps a sales outlet to improve its on-the-spot service and sales, can be communicated by letter.

Word processors make it easy to personalise sales letters by allowing names, addresses and variable information to be inserted and printed out individually, which is preferable to photocopied or duplicated letters. If you are not able, or not prepared, to do the job in-house a word-processing bureau will do it for you.

The distribution list for sales letters should be classified and maintained separately from lists kept for other purposes – direct mail or press releases for example.

Action guide

- Make sure that your sales letters *look* like personal letters, not circulars. Use the company's standard letterhead, address each one to an individual and sign it.
- Write courteously and succinctly. Avoid advertising jargon ('unique opportunity', 'special offer', etc). Point out an advantage or emphasise a distinct benefit to the recipient.
- Match style and content to recipients.
- Invite response by asking a question, or offering additional information. Make it easy to respond by giving a name and telephone number, or enclosing a simple form or reply-paid card.

- Consider follow-up letters, but do not send out sales letters too lightly; this medium can be over-used: it is an extension of, not a substitute for, other forms of advertising.
- Do not write sales letters too frequently, or just because it seems to be about time you distributed one.
- Keep a copy of all sales letters and the distribution list.

CHAPTER 5
Mailing Lists

Mailing lists are essential for direct mail and sales letters. They may be compiled in-house, rented or purchased. Which is chosen depends mainly on availability and the nature, target and size of the mailing. In-house list management is a chore, but good lists are extremely valuable. Once in existence they should not be made accessible to unauthorised examination. Creating one's own lists is easiest when the required data already exists in a manageable form, for example on a computer database, word processor or other files which are well maintained and can be searched, examined, updated and amended.

Under the Data Protection Act all computerised lists containing names, addresses and other personal data must be registered and available for inspection by any member of the public on demand. Holders of such lists are also required by the Act to amend or delete entries if requested to do so. Details of the Act and how it could affect you are obtainable from the Office of the Data Protection Registrar, Springfield House, Water Lane, Wilmslow, Cheshire SK9 5AX.

A Code of Practice Covering the Use of Personal Data for Advertising and Direct Marketing Purposes is available from the Advertising Association, Abford House, 15 Wilton Road, London SW1V 1NJ. It was prepared in the interests of self-regulation by list users, and is endorsed by the Data Protection Registrar.

Your own sales records are the best foundation on which to

build mailing lists, though it will probably be necessary to add and reclassify data, and remove duplications. You will probably not want to use the whole list for every mailing and it is useful to be able to access defined parts of it for specific purposes. Sources for mailing lists include:

1. Existing customers, sales contacts and enquiries, correspondence and advertising response coupons.
2. Membership lists and directories of business, trade and professional organisations, clubs, societies and chambers of commerce. Official handbooks, year-books and similar annual publications are useful, but often seriously out of date for mailing purposes.
3. Classified public directories, eg Yellow Pages, regional handbooks and guides.

Keep in mind that every list is out of date, virtually from the moment it is produced. Even recently published lists can be seriously inaccurate. From whatever sources lists are derived, regular and conscientious 'cleaning' will be necessary.

It is preferable, though not always feasible, to use only named addressees. Bear this in mind, even if the source list does not supply all the information needed to address communications personally. Maybe you can gradually improve the list in this respect from internal knowledge and experience. If so it's worth doing.

Buying and renting lists

There are several ways of acquiring existing lists. Some publications sell their circulation lists and produce a list catalogue. In most cases, publishers who sell or rent lists also provide a mailing service. If so the advertiser may, for a charge, obtain a complete service for addressing, insertion and distribution. This is neat provided you can be reasonably sure that the list is well targeted for your particular mail shot.

Another way of acquiring lists is from list brokers, who do not maintain their own lists but have a knowledge of, and access to, lists over a wide and selective range of market sectors. Brokers should belong to the British List Brokers Association, the members of which comply with a Code of Practice. A BLBA members' list is available from the Association at Springfield House, Princess Street, Bristol BS3 4EF, telephone 0272 666900.

Some brokers specialise. Most are knowledgeable in their fields and can extract names and addresses for very precisely identified categories (eg car owners and people in specific professions) and for specific age brackets, social groups and income profiles. This is called 'psychographic' ('what they do') listing. Demographic ('where they live') lists are also readily available in many classifications, from neighbourhoods upwards.

The precise targeting which well-classified lists permit is a powerful tool for direct mail users. It is better to make a number of separate, well-targeted mailings than a single 'blanket' mailing, and classified lists are also useful for small test mailings.

The acid test for every list is whether it has recently been 'cleaned' and can therefore be considered substantially up to date. There is unfortunately no way of being certain about this until you have used it. As a precaution, find out when the list was last rented before buying it. If it was some time ago its accuracy is suspect. Spot-check a few names or addresses which you know, and expect to find in it. This could provide a clue to whether it is likely to be worth what it costs.

The cost of buying or renting lists depends on their size, psychographic and demographic selectivity and exclusivity. Prices are usually calculated per 1000 names. Companies which specialise in the contract production of direct mail packages will either have their own lists or have access to suitable lists on their clients' behalf.

The Mailing Preference Service is a non-profit-making organisation supported by the Post Office for the regulation of direct response advertising. Subscribers undertake to use only MPS-cleaned lists, which are updated every three months. At present the MPS is concerned only with the rental of consumer lists and does not operate for business list users.

It also provides a service for consumers who want their names removed from direct mail lists.

Useful information on lists, and other aspects of direct mail, is available from the Post Office's Area Sales Offices which are shown under Post Office Services in telephone directories.

Action guide

- Build and manage your own mailing lists if at all possible, even if you occasionally rent or buy lists. Use every source of list building and list cleaning you can find – customer records, sales reports and enquiries, advertisement response forms, warranty cards, etc. Comb directories for new names.
- Clean, prune and update lists frequently and regularly. Make somebody directly responsible for doing it or do it yourself.
- Keep lists private and secure; they are valuable. If they are held on computer protect them from accidental erasure and unauthorised use.
- Subdivide, classify and cross-reference your main (source) list into as many categories as may be necessary to target your mailings.
- After every mailing monitor postal returns for deletions and changes in names, job titles and addresses. Then clean your lists again!
- Before you buy a list, ask questions about it and try to spot-check its accuracy, preferably before, or otherwise as soon as possible after you pay for it.
- If you use outside services for production and despatch ensure that you make clear how, where and when the mailing list will be available.
- For advice and guidance contact the organisations already mentioned in this chapter, and those listed on pp 52–3.

CHAPTER 6
Point of Sale

Advertising displayed, or made available, where the advertised product or service can be bought or obtained is called point-of-sale (POS) advertising. By definition, POS is more likely to be used at retail outlets than elsewhere, though this need not always be intended to produce immediate sales. For example, travel agencies use a large amount of POS in the form of displays and brochures to help people to choose their holidays.

When planning POS the advertiser must take carefully into account the conditions which exist at the outlet, and practicalities such as the amount of space available, the number of outlets, the size and durability of displays, the amount of 'customer traffic' and the level of sales support and competitive advertising at the POS. These factors alone – and there may be others – will determine fairly accurately what form POS advertising should take and what results it is likely to produce.

Free-standing displays can be expensive to design, produce and maintain, and their effectiveness will rely on their being positioned effectively. In press or poster advertising the advertiser 'rents' the space which an advertisement occupies; but if the space occupied by POS is not owned or rented by the advertiser the effectiveness of the display will further depend on whether the outlet is able and willing to display it.

Ambitious POS displays call on creative skills and resources to produce. If these are not available in-house they can be bought from specialist display designers and manufacturers, who should also be able to advise on the most effective and economical solutions to specified requirements.

The value of POS in attracting attention and providing information where buying decisions are made is sufficiently high to encourage its use wherever it stands a good chance of supporting advertising in other media. Before embarking on specially designed POS, existing print, such as brochures, catalogues, leaflets, etc, should be reviewed for possible use at a POS. For example, placing a product catalogue where people can easily examine and obtain it has obvious benefits, including low-cost distribution. Brochures, house journals, press releases and other items which advertise or promote the company and its products, including perhaps trade journals which carry the company's advertising, may also be used as POS material in places where customers, potential customers or the general public are likely to be present. Retail premises are, by their nature, 'points of sale', but reception areas, waiting rooms, sales departments and, indeed, anywhere else that business is being transacted, could be appropriate for a POS display.

When deciding what form a display should take careful attention must be paid to its location and what is likely to be happening there. Notices, stick-on labels, three-dimensional displays, posters, leaflets and brochures all attract attention in different ways. It might also be necessary to decide whether a POS display will provide information or be used for purely promotional display purposes. In supermarkets or chain stores POS displays are seen by large numbers of people, but they compete for attention and must be capable of claiming it in an in-store environment. In more controlled, less active environments it is easier to claim attention, provided the material is well placed and interesting.

A wide variety of manufactured display modules and receptacles are available from stationery shops and display materials dealers, or can be made to measure by display designers and manufacturers. They can then be over-printed with a company's name, or an advertising message, or used unprinted simply to hold POS material and keep it tidy.

Action guide

- Make sure at the design and production stages that POS material will be suited to the conditions and requirements of the locations where it will be displayed.
- Ensure that POS displays are designed and constructed for easy transportation and erection.
- Use durable materials for semi-permanent, and especially outdoor, displays so that they do not deteriorate quickly and look tatty.
- Spot-check POS displays *in situ* to see whether they are being used properly.
- If take-away items such as catalogues or brochures are used make sure that there is always enough available. Monitor call-off so that the display can be replenished quickly. Make it clear to the public that the items may be taken away and are free.
- Relate the amount and variety of POS material to the environment in which it will be displayed. A take-away leaflet in a busy, active environment can be more effective than an elaborate static display.

CHAPTER 7
Exhibitions

Exhibitions are primarily selling, rather than advertising, orientated; but since the public – including customers and potential customers – is present, advertising cannot be neglected. Exhibition advertising is divided into:

- Pre-exhibition advertising
- Advertising and promotion at the exhibition
- Post-exhibition advertising.

Exhibition space is booked well in advance and the run-up time before the opening date should be used to prepare and produce what's needed, avoiding any last-minute rush. In most cases new advertisements will have to be created and produced. Ideally, advertising requirements should be anticipated and scheduled as soon as a decision is made to participate in an exhibition or similar event, and made part of the advertising budget for that period. Advertising directly connected with the event can then be properly costed. If unbudgeted money is used for this purpose the advertising budget should be amended to include it.

Press advertising linked to exhibitions where a company will show its products or services supplements the mainstream advertising effort. Newspapers and magazines which publish special features, or complete issues, containing exhibition previews usually offer special rates to participants. If space is taken the advertiser should produce ads which stimulate the interest of readers likely to attend, and not be content with bald 'we'll see you there' statements.

It is not unusual for 'editorial support' to be offered to advertisers in special exhibition features of this kind. It is worth the effort to provide what's asked for when advertising is booked (see Advertising Features, pp 30–31). Writing editorial material is journalism or public relations, rather than an advertising activity, but you will probably be told what's wanted. Alternatively, it may be written by a staff journalist from information which you supply.

It is well to be alert to opportunities for making contact with journalists at exhibitions (the advertising reps will probably need no encouragement!). Exhibition organisers sometimes offer press liaison facilities as a service to exhibitors. If so, find out what they are and how to use them. Verbal information, captioned photographs and press releases on the company's products could be in demand for editorial pre-exhibition features, and during the show by reporters covering it. Make sure that you know what's wanted. Most exhibitions have press offices where exhibitors can leave information in the form of brochures and press releases.

All catalogues, leaflets, brochures, etc, required at the exhibition should be up to date, and available in the quantities needed, well before the exhibition. If this means re-ordering regularly used printed materials, or updating them to coincide with the event, the cost of doing so should be part of the advertising budget. Indeed, there might be an argument for allocating *all* the overhead costs of participation in exhibitions to the advertising and promotion budget.

If advertisements are placed in the exhibition catalogue, or posters produced for display within the exhibition, bear in mind that an exhibition is only a temporary market-place and these ads will be effective only for as long as it lasts. Advertising directly linked to your company's participation should be attention-getting, ie attract people to your stand and stimulate interest or curiosity in what is being shown there.

Follow-up advertising after exhibitions has its uses. Since the exhibition is over and the captive audience dispersed, it calls for a different approach from pre-exhibition advertising.

Sales successes, the appointment of new agencies and other business matters could suggest new advertisements. Press reports provide further opportunities for related advertising along the lines I have already suggested for pre-exhibition advertising.

Stand space, stand erection, display and other overheads are outside the scope of this book, except to note that visitors form an impression of your company from what they see and how they are received at an exhibition stand, so the stand should be more than simply a display area. It is a business environment which the company creates for itself; a place where people meet, talk, ask questions and move around. In design and presentation the stand should be conducive to doing business and communicating information. Make sure that some arrangement is made to record the names, addresses and business titles of visitors. These will be useful for, among other things, list building and cleaning.

A good basic guide to exhibiting is John Talbot's *How to Make Exhibitions Work for your Business*, a Daily Telegraph guide published by Kogan Page.

CHAPTER 8
Recruitment Advertising

Recruitment advertising should be seen as an integral part of your overall advertising policy and, as such, receive its due attention. If a recruitment ad does not attract suitable applicants a portion of the budget is wasted and the company loses a unique opportunity for meeting qualified people.

Recruitment advertising should focus not only on vacancies, but also on the perceived priorities and interests of the applicants who could fill them. Yet again I have to say that if you don't know what you want from an ad it's hard to produce a good one. Questions such as, 'Where is the person who could fill this vacancy likely to be, and what is he or she likely to be doing when they see the ad?' are basic. Then ask 'What could persuade them to apply for this vacancy rather than another?'

A recruitment ad should offer more than bare details: the company's working environment, and its attitude to people who work for it, are conveyed by recruitment advertising. Remember, too, that recruitment ads can be read by your employees and could affect the way your existing staff feel about their work. They are also seen by customers and competitors, which could affect the way they regard your company. Try to convey that yours is a company which values its employees.

Classified semi-display ads are the usual medium for recruitment advertising. Allow yourself all the space you need to say what you want, and pay careful attention to

> **JKL (UK) LTD**
> *A DIRECT LINE TO CAREER SUCCESS*
> £00,000 p.a.   DIRECT MARKETING EXECUTIVE
>
> JKL is the UK arm of a highly successful international supplier of kitchen goods. We are committed to substantial investment in our already extensive direct marketing operations, and need an experienced marketer to take responsibility for the direct marketing of two of our premier brands of cooking utensils and tableware.
>
> Reporting to the Sales and Marketing Manager, you will be responsible for planning, implementing and monitoring direct mail campaigns to both the retail and domestic markets. You will have at least two years' experience of direct mail marketing in the FMCG sector, which will have given you a thorough knowledge of direct mail packaging and production techniques. An ability to brief and work closely with creative and production staff is essential, as is experience of managing a direct mail budget.
>
> This is a post which offers a significant career progression for the right candidate, as well as all the benefits associated with a large company. To apply, please send your CV to .... , Personnel Manager, JKL (UK) Ltd, Friar House, Westhampton.

Figure 8.1 *Semi-display classified recruitment ad*

**EXPERIENCED
DATA ENTRY CLERK**
required for Easthampton- based mail order company. Duties include updating and sorting direct mail lists using dBase 3 on an IBM PS2. Accurate keyboard skills and high level of concentration essential, database experience an advantage but full training given. Further involvement in sales/marketing possible in due course. £0,000 p.a. Benefits include pension scheme, canteen and staff discounts. Please write to .... Personnel Manager, XYZ Ltd, Catalogue House, Easthampton, for an application form.

Figure 8.2 *Classified recruitment ad*

Reproduced from *Readymade Job Advertisements* (Kogan Page, 1991)
by kind permission of the author

design and typography as well as to copywriting. Your ad will appear with others in the same classification and it should stand up to them in terms of appearance and presentation. (A recruitment ad can be made an exercise in producing camera-ready copy (see pp 101–2).) It is always worth noticing how other advertisers, especially your competitors, try to attract staff. Critically assess such recruitment advertising and compare it with your own, then ask yourself what sort of people you think would apply for what's on offer.

Of course, the actual copy depends largely on what's required, but in recruitment advertising it is invariably better to use more rather than fewer words if, by doing so, you tell applicants something they need to know when deciding whether to apply. Copy should be relaxed and informative. Personally, I do not like quirky or jokey copy in recruitment advertising, though an ad seeking a receptionist will obviously need to differ in style as well as content from one looking for a lion tamer. If you have a clear mental picture of the kind of applicant you want you are some way towards working out how best to attract an application.

Action guide

- A recruitment ad should include the company's name and the name of someone to whom applications should be sent, a clear job description, if possible a salary range, any particular requirements such as work experience and educational qualifications, and an address or telephone number where intending applicants can, without obligation, find out more about the job. I have read many recruitment ads which omit one or other of these.
- Take care not to flout the laws of racial or sexual discrimination. If you do, even unintentionally, the outcome could be damaging and expensive. If in doubt about the wording of a recruitment ad in this respect the publication's advertising department, or your legal adviser, will be able to provide guidance.

- Fringe benefits and amenities, such as a pensions scheme, a staff restaurant or a private car park, are worth mentioning if only to show that your company is considerate enough to provide them.
- For senior staff consider hitherto untried media, such as professional journals and local newspapers outside your area. Test them with one or two ads and monitor results.
- If you advertise the same vacancy in more than one place always identify the source from which the best applications come – it will be a useful guide for future recruitment advertising.
- Run-of-the-mill copy attracts run-of-the-mill applicants. Think how you would talk to an applicant face to face; how you would set out to interest and enthuse a prospective member of your staff.
- If you invite telephone enquiries make sure that someone will be available to deal with them in a friendly, informative way.
- Give yourself as much time as possible to process applications and fill the position without haste and inconvenience, either to yourself or your applicant. If, as is likely, a successful applicant is already employed take into account possible delays, such as contractual obligations to an existing employer or the need to move to a new area.
- Deal with lower-grade vacancies as carefully, courteously and considerately as with higher and management grades.

CHAPTER 9
Premiums and Promotions

A premium offer is an inducement to promote business. A promotional offer reminds customers and potential customers of a company's name and its products or services. The former usually has strings attached; the latter should have none.

Premiums

You are not in business to give things away for nothing and most people are well aware of this, so premiums must be judged carefully. Focus on what the offer will cost in relation to what it aims to produce in terms of response. In addition to the intrinsic cost of whatever is offered, the cost of making a premium offer includes promoting it through advertising or direct mail, distribution and handling and, in most cases, a follow-up mailing.

Premium offers are commonplace in mainstream direct mail, where experience indicates fairly precisely what they could be, and what they can and cannot be expected to accomplish. For example, book clubs offer certain books at bargain prices in return for an undertaking to buy further books, and the cost of such offers is set against the additional profits they bring from the new members they attract. Similarly, if a 'free gift' persuades a sufficient number of people to buy a magazine which they might otherwise not have bought the resulting circulation increase is worth having, especially if it leads to an increase in advertising

revenue. Premium offers made to secure an increased customer base over the longer or shorter term are therefore
successful when they are liquidated by the *marginally* added
sales, and repeat sales, which they can produce.

What is offered and to whom it is offered depends, as usual,
on the product or service and its potential market. If that
market is limited and well defined a significantly large
number of new customers might not be reached through a
premium offer, though it could still be justified if it draws
attention to products or services which can then be converted
into sales or heighten the advertiser's market profile.

Conditions may be set on who is eligible to apply for a
premium offer, but if it is advertised as 'free' you will be
expected to supply whatever is offered without cost and
unconditionally to anyone entitled to receive it.

It should go without saying that a premium should be
attractive enough to interest people who might not otherwise
respond, and must be supported by advertising. The easiest
and neatest solution is to discount the full cost of a product or
service for a specified period, eg by offering a discounted pre-
publication price for an expensive book or a significant price
reduction for a limited period on a product or service. In the
case of new or relaunched products a premium offer is not
only a sales stimulant but also a valuable marketing tool, in
that it can indicate fairly accurately the level of sales that can
be expected when the product or service is offered to a wider
market without a premium inducement.

Promotions

Promotions are easy to handle. Note pads, pens, key-rings
and other useful trinkets, or more expensive presents, such as
briefcases and travelling clocks, can be selected from the
catalogues of companies which specialise in supplying suitable promotional items and arranging for them to be marked
or printed with a company name, logo or advertising message. This type of promotion is indeed 'bread on the waters'
advertising insofar as it can rarely be shown directly to

influence buying decisions. In some situations, however, promotional advertising can be effective in calculable ways.

As a buyer of print I receive diaries, calendars, wall charts, magnifiers and other things which, in use, serve to keep the names of the suppliers who produce them available when needed. The printed plastic bags produced, and sometimes sold, by supermarkets and other retailers are so useful that shoppers do not seem to mind becoming walking advertisements for the stores which provide them. The criterion is, of course, utility. If expensively produced print, such as illustrated calendars, is distributed it should be attractive enough, and practical enough, to be used as such. Personally, when I look at a calendar I want to see the date easily and quickly, not to examine a landscape or, much less, admire an unclothed girl.

Useful addresses

Incentive Today
Langfords Publications Ltd, 32 West Street, Brighton
BN1 2RT; 0273 206722

Institute of Sales Promotion
Arena House, 66–68 Pentonville Road, London N1 9HS;
071-837 5340

Promotional Handling Association
Arena House, 66–68 Pentonville Road, London N1 9HS;
071-837 5340

Sales Promotion Consultants Association
Arena House, 66–68 Pentonville Road, London N1 9HS;
071-837 5340

CHAPTER 10
Creating Advertisements

The role of agencies and services

The creative side of advertising is linked with production requirements: it is not only pointless to create advertisements which do not meet the needs of your advertising plan and help to fulfil its purpose, but also a waste of time to produce advertising unsuited to the medium in which it will appear. The most original and ingenious ads are useless if they do not meet these criteria. Companies managing their own advertising need to know exactly what creative and production resources are available and how to use them. Production is dealt with in some detail later. Here I am concerned mainly with initiating and creating advertisements.

With the help of this book it should be possible to put a useful range of advertising into effect; but if your plan (to say nothing of your budget!) runs to major press campaigns, TV, posters, large direct mail packages or similarly ambitious projects you will not be able to do everything for yourself, and the only sensible course is to get professional assistance. Even modest advertising plans can benefit from the help an advertising agency or consultant can give. It is for you to decide whether you need it and, if so, how to find it.

Many small advertising agencies provide useful, well-defined services, but locating the one which is right for you could take time. First, list and visit local agencies. Being reasonably near to your agency promotes good liaison and quick communications.

Discuss your plans in detail at senior level, and talk to the people – art directors, copy chiefs, media buyers and others – who are directly responsible for running the agency's services. If an agency appears interested and enthusiastic about your advertising ask questions which could help you to decide whether it is right for your company's needs, such as:

- How long has it been in existence?
- Exactly what services does it claim to provide, and are they available internally?
- How many full-time staff does it have, and what are their duties and qualifications?
- What other advertising accounts does the agency service?
- Has it any experience in your particular market?
- How does the agency structure its charges to clients?

Be prepared to discuss your budget, and any existing or projected advertising. Ask to see specimens of work done by the agency. Personal impressions also count: do the people at the agency look, talk and act like professionals? Will they listen to what *you* have to say as well as tell you what *they* think? If your company becomes a client you or members of your staff will be dealing on a one-to-one basis with agency personnel.

An agency is there to work for you, but it cannot think for you. A company still needs to be active in planning and initiating its advertising. Explain to the agency what you believe you are able to do for yourself, especially in the areas of preparation and origination. Agency-prepared roughs, visuals and alternative presentations increase creative costs and might not be necessary. When you know what services are available, identify those you think you will need, and can afford.

Small agencies can become an important creative and production ancillary to a company's advertising effort, with one important proviso: it is unwise, and unfair, to employ an agency simply to carry out routine chores. If an agency is not allowed to discuss, advise and become involved in the immediate and longer-term advertising objectives of a client it will not want to retain that client's account. If you intend to supply camera-ready copy or artwork, or buy any creative or production services externally, say so; do not do so without the agency's knowledge. If you are honest and open with an agency you stand a good chance of getting what you pay for.

Agency costs

Most agencies' income is derived from commission based on the advertising they place on behalf of their clients (usually between 10 and 15 per cent of net cost) plus a commission (around 20 per cent) on all the materials and services needed to prepare and produce a client's advertising, ie the overheads required to service an account. Large agencies handle high-budget accounts. Small agencies with clients whose advertising expenditure is insufficient to produce much revenue on a commission basis may also charge a fixed yearly fee agreed with the client. However they are structured, agency fees are usually good value for money. In addition to the services and facilities it provides an agency can bargain on advertising costs on its clients' behalf and optimise what they get for what they spend.

The alternative

The alternative to using an advertising agency is to find out what services are immediately available, or can be acquired, in-house, and be prepared to buy in any additional ones needed to carry out your advertising as planned.

Creative services, such as copywriting, design and artwork to professional standards, are not cheap to obtain, and it can also be difficult to locate people with the skills, and knowledge of your markets, necessary to produce good results.

Production and distribution services, such as printing, typesetting, list rental and materials, are discussed in more detail under their respective headings. The most sensible general advice is to cut your advertising coat according to your cloth, explore your existing potential and take full advantage of all the help you can get, and afford, along the way.

Copywriting

The acid test of copy – which, in advertising, includes headlines – is whether it supports the intentions of the advertiser. The copy must present the advertiser's message attractively, clearly and persuasively. To do this it must not only command attention, but also sustain attention for long enough to convey its message. Every word of copy should be there for a reason and be *seen* to be working for its keep: however elegant, entertaining or apt copy may look when drafted these conditions must always take priority.

Before drafting copy the writer needs to know a good deal about the company and the product or service advertised, the medium in which the advertisement will appear and the target readership. The last mentioned implies a clear and, as far as possible, detailed mental concept of the kind of readers who will see the ad, and the context in which it is likely to be read. The copywriter needs answers to questions like these:

- *Where* will the ad appear?
- *What* is its purpose?
- *What* sort of person will read it?
- *How* can I attract and hold his or her attention?
- *What* response am I looking for?

Think in terms of 'a reader' rather than 'a readership'. The ad may be seen by thousands – even millions – of people, but whoever reads it receives a direct, personal communication from the advertiser. So, just as we do not talk to individuals as though they were an anonymous crowd, we should address advertisements to just one reader – a preoccupied reader who might well be about to look elsewhere or think of other things and, what's more, is neither obliged to read your ad nor to take any notice of its message.

It is obvious that an ad must attract attention, but it is not so obvious that attention must also be held for long enough to assimilate the advertiser's message. Many ads succeed in the first requirement, but fail in the second. Clever graphics, slogans and amusing or intriguing headlines may arouse interest, but they rarely do the whole job.

Copywriters must also face the fact that attention span can often be measured in split seconds, and that it's easy to see something without assimilating it. They should resist the temptation to try to make the copy do too much. To get a clear and believable message well and truly home is the prime objective. If, for example, low price, high quality and quick delivery are all valid claims it may be necessary to decide which is the most important in that particular ad.

The copywriter also needs to know how much space is available for copy, and how it relates to the overall layout of the ad. A vague 'here be copy' indication is not enough. A visual (see p 92) or a complete layout helps to define the copy areas fairly precisely. It is far better to write copy to a known length than to 'let it find its own length', or dicker around with it at proof stage to try to make it fit.

Concise copy is preferable, but remember that people are prepared to read ads which they find sufficiently interesting or intriguing; not every ad demands short copy, as many successful campaigns demonstrate. The medium, the target readership and the advertiser's intentions combine to indicate how much copy will be desirable, though the longer the copy the more the demands made on copywriting skills.

When drafting copy, take your time and do not be satisfied too quickly. Read draft copy carefully and critically. Try reading it aloud: if it doesn't *sound* convincing it probably won't be convincing in print. Draft and re-draft.

Professional copywriters refer to 'tracking', which means copy which moves easily and convincingly from one point to the next and thereby holds a reader's interest from start to finish. Does your copy 'track'? If you suspect that anything in it is likely to bore, puzzle or irritate the reader don't waste time defending it – cut it out!

A critical analysis of other people's advertising, especially that of your competitors, is good training for copywriting.

Ask yourself what *they* are trying to do. Then whether you think they are doing it effectively. Could you do better? If so how? Don't simply imitate them – learn from them.

Every penny spent on advertising counts, so look critically at inspirations – unusual, oddball or humorous ideas which strike you while you are writing. Originality is by no means to be spurned, but the copy must actively support the advertiser's intention. In one of the most widely admired campaigns of the past a trade organisation of hatters used the slogan 'If you want to get ahead, get a hat', which is crisp and amusing; but it failed to sell many hats!

Headlines attract attention and stimulate interest. Body copy conveys a message. Here are some general copywriting guidelines:

- Be wary of over-emphasis through underlining, capitalisation, italics and exclamation marks. Copy should communicate on a personal level, which means it is better not to shout your advertising message.
- Prefer what looks and sounds convincing to what seems clever.
- Write as though you have only a short time to say what you want to say.
- Do not be pompous or obscure. Do not exaggerate or strain after slick effects. Avoid sloganising and advertising hype.
- Be consistent.
- Do not make unsupported claims or 'knock' your competitors.
- Treat the reader as a busy, intelligent human being, not an audience to be addressed from a platform.
- Write clearly, simply and grammatically. Use short sentences. Punctuate correctly, but do not over-punctuate. Punctuation is not needed in headlines, whatever current typographical fashion may dictate in this respect.
- Prefer positive to negative statements: 'Do it now' is a positive statement; 'Why not do it now?' is not.
- Don't use words like 'great', 'outstanding', 'remarkable', 'first class' just to zip up the ad. Say what you mean, and

make it read as though you mean what you say. If something is 'guaranteed' say what it's guaranteed to do (or not to do).

- Copywriters should read proofs, but proof stage is not the time for rethinking copy. Errors must be corrected and small alterations which improve the ad can sometimes be made in proof, but don't count on it.

Captions

Captions are essential positively to identify photographs and any other illustrations throughout the creative and production stages. Uncaptioned photographs and unidentifiable artwork have a high disaster potential. However 'obvious' it may look, a caption which states precisely what the illustration shows should always be attached (preferably with adhesive tape, never with a pin, staple or paper clip and not with gum, which can cause chemical staining) to the back of photographs, and on the overlay of artwork. This is especially important when, as frequently happens, a number of similar photographs or illustrations are present, only one of which will be selected for use in the published ad.

A simple numerical or alphabetical key can be used as a unique identification for each picture (eg, 1 Car. Side view A, 2 Car. Side view B, 3 Car. Front view A, etc). Provided the list of keyed captions is always kept with the set there should then be no doubt which caption refers to which photograph or illustration at every stage up to and beyond publication.

There is frequently no need for printed captions in published advertisements, but designers, copywriters and production staff must know beyond doubt what illustrations are to be used. Designers must be able to select and identify the required illustration, and unless the required illustrations and layout of an ad are known it is difficult for a copywriter to estimate exactly how much space is available for copy and how it could appear in context. Finally, when the origination goes forward for production it will be handled by people who have never seen it before. Here clear, unambiguous captioning is a safeguard against expensive, and possibly irretrievable, errors being made at this important stage.

Advertising design

The very word 'design' can lead to confusion. Design is certainly a creative activity, but not exclusively; it must take account of ways and means, function and purpose, which means that some compromises are necessary. *Every* item of print has to be designed by someone. Even if all that is wanted is a single word on a page, at some point somebody has to decide in what size, in what typeface and where on the page it should appear. Advertising design, in this sense, is less a matter of pure creativity than of judging what is feasible and appropriate. Design is important to every ad, and particularly so if it contains a large amount of text or graphics.

Though advertising design calls on many skills, and some professional specialisations, the advertiser should be aware of its significance and be prepared to cultivate a response to advertising in terms of its appearance as well as its content.

For example, an advertised list of vehicles offered for sale by a car dealer has to be arranged and presented in a specified space. Exactly how the list will appear when typeset can be decided by the advertiser, by a professional typographic designer, by the advertising department of the publication in which it will appear, or even by the typesetter who sets the ad. Whoever does it will be responsible for design. Copywriting and artwork are heavily dependent for their effectiveness on how they are presented.

A glance at a page of semi-display advertising will show that some ads are more attractive and easier to read than others. The readable, and therefore more effective, ads are simply better designed than the rest. Even a basic understanding of typography, design and layout can go a long way towards improving the impact of your advertising. Here are some specimen typefaces.

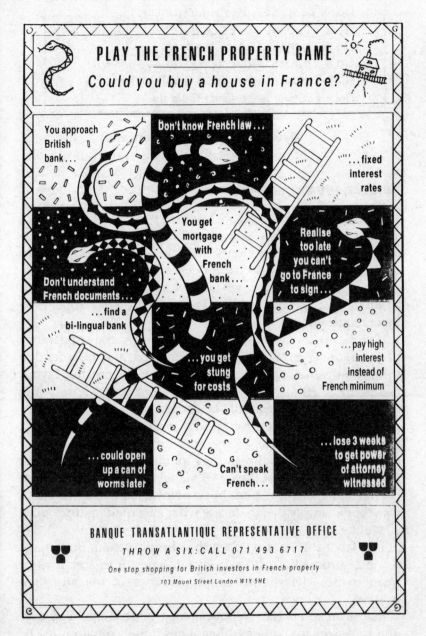

Figure 10.1 *An intriguing advertisement which attracts immediate attention*

Do It Yourself Advertising (roman)
Do It Yourself Advertising (roman sanserif)
Do It Yourself Advertising (italic)
Do It Yourself Advertising (italic sanserif)
Do It Yourself Advertising (bold)
Do It Yourself Advertising (bold italic)

Figure 10.2 *Examples of typefaces*

Visuals, roughs and layouts

Roughs are sometimes called 'visuals', but it is useful to make a distinction. Visuals are design concepts – visual representations of how advertisements *could* be laid out, but open to choice, discussion and change. An advertising agency may produce a number of visuals which the advertiser can compare and choose the one which most closely appears to meet requirements.

Roughs are made at the stage when the general appearance of an ad, or series of ads, has been decided, and are intended to show how they will look when laid out. The finished layout is a plan, or guide, which indicates more precisely how the designer's intentions should be carried out.

To make a rough it is first necessary to know the sizes and shapes of all the parts of the ad which must ultimately be fitted together as headlines, copy, photographs and graphics, and the overall size of the ad. A visual or rough can easily be changed and manipulated, but a point will be reached when somebody simply has to decide what's wanted, and produce a layout.

The layout is an advanced, but by no means final stage towards production. It is, in effect, a set of instructions or 'map' which determines the appearance of the ad when printed.

Before an acceptable layout can be produced, the typefaces and typesizes for copy and headlines it will contain must be decided (see pp 88–9), together with the dimensions of all artwork or photographs as they will appear: nothing can be left out if it is to be part of the published ad.

When typefaces and sizes are being chosen it is fairly easy to find out whether they will fit the amount of space they must occupy. This is called a cast-off, and can be done by counting all characters and spaces and referring to a type specimen which gives an accurate count of the number of characters in a given point-size (or in metric measurements) in a given measure (length of line). The points system of type measurement is complicated and inconsistent, and metric measurements are easier to use. Tracing large type for headlines from a specimen and placing the tracing directly on to the layout is a painstaking, but accurate, way of measuring exactly how much space a headline will occupy *in situ*.

For small spaces with no illustrations less precision is needed. For body copy (text) 20 words per square inch in 10-point type, or 30 words in 8-point, is a rough guide. (Below that you ought to be asking whether it is not too small to read easily!) The measure (length) of lines as well as their depth must, of course, be taken into account. If, on a layout, the copy simply cannot be made to fit the space available for it the only remedy is to edit it until it does.

After a layout has been produced a typeset proof will show *exactly* how it will appear in print. The proof is your final opportunity to correct or amend a layout, but it is time-wasting to demand a completely new layout unless a serious or obvious error has been made, since the expense of typesetting has already been incurred.

If either camera-ready copy (crc) or camera-ready artwork (cra) is prepared in-house more layout skills will be called for. The preparation of crc and cra can usually be regarded as a production rather than a creative task, and is discussed in Chapter 11.

Action guide

- Decide how far you can confidently go in preparing your own visuals, roughs and layouts. If you have agency or professional assistance use it, or get skilled help whenever possible; but acquire a critical eye. Learn from experience, evaluate the appearance of your own ads, and compare them with others of a similar size and purpose in the same medium.

- Use consistent measurements which have been agreed with, and will therefore be followed, by whoever is handling and processing the ad for publication.
- Know the exact sizes of all the spaces you book, and use a system of measurements which you understand, and is understood by your printer or the publisher's advertising department.
- Ask for guidance on the typefaces and sizes available from the printer or publisher who is handling the ad, and obtain specimen alphabets and settings, preferably of advertisements similar to those you have in mind.
- Make visuals and roughs as realistic as you can, but do not be too easily satisfied by them.
- Take into account the medium as well as the ad.
- Use space creatively. Crowded ads are less attractive than harmoniously balanced ones.
- If you have to change copy to fit layout consult the copywriter to make sure that you can do so without reducing its effectiveness. Sometimes changing a single word, or punctuation mark, is enough to solve the problem. It might also be possible to reduce the sizes of type used, provided this will not interfere with legibility.

Single-colour photographs and line work

Black-and-white (continuous tone) photographs are prepared for printing by the halftone process, which involves re-photographing them with the introduction of a screen which breaks the tones of the original into areas of dots, from the lightest to the darkest, the largest dots being in the dark areas and the smallest in the light ones. This is called *screening*. All so-called 'black-and-white' photographs are therefore printed in graduated shades from black through grey to white. This, combined with the printing process and the paper on which

Figure 10.3 *Screened halftone. Enlarged, a screened halftone is seen to be a pattern of dots. The lighter areas are made up of black dots on a white ground and the darker, shaded areas of larger black dots.*

they are printed, inevitably reduces sharpness and contrast compared with the original.

Half-tone screens are measured in dots per inch (actually dots per inch square) or per centimetre; 133 dpi equals 54 dpc. Screens can be coarse or fine, depending on the subject and the paper to be used. In dpi, 150 screen is about the finest in commercial use, though for very high-fidelity reproduction screens as fine as 200 and 300 may be used. Photographs printed on reasonably good paper, such as those used for books and magazines, use 133 to 150 screen, and newspaper photographs can be as low as 56.

Certain other effects can be produced either before or after the repro (reproduction) stage. *Vignetting*, which gives an appearance of fading towards the edges of the photograph, can be done by special screens or directly on to the original, as can *airbrushing* which obliterates any part of a photograph not required for reproduction.

Most tonal drawings, such as pencil drawings, are treated as halftones to produce their varying shades. The dots (tones) can then be 'dropped out' of non-image-bearing areas so that only the underlying paper will be visible. There are many ways of producing artistic effects in black-and-white reproduction, but it is necessary to know how a drawing will be printed before these are undertaken. Consultation with a printer will soon establish whether an effect can be reproduced as required.

Single-colour line work, which includes drawn or transfer lettering, is easily reproduced, though fine lines print well only on good quality papers. Though artwork can be enlarged or reduced for printing, it is preferable to present it 'same size' (the actual size needed) if this is practicable, so that a visual estimate can be made of its reproduction potential.

Spot colour

Colour does not automatically improve an ad. If colour is used it should make the ad more distinctive or attractive, otherwise it's a waste of money. Try to visualise how it will appear in colour and in print, remembering that paper and the technical requirements of the printing process both have a considerable influence on colour reproduction. Given good originals, modern colour printing technology is capable of remarkably faithful results, but since colour invariably attracts a higher cost than monochrome the extra expense ought to be justifiable on more solid grounds than personal preference.

A distinction must be made between process ('full') colour, which produces a wide range of colours, as is needed to reproduce colour artwork or colour photographs (see p 97), and 'spot colour', where small areas of colour can be printed in defined places ('spots') on a page, eg for text, headlines, borders or decorations. In newspapers and magazines where it is available spot colour is usually available only on certain pages.

Spot colour is printed as a solid (an unbroken area of colour), though tints can be introduced which break up the solid with textured patterns of lines, dots, etc, which reduce its intensity.

Spot colour is widely available in newspapers and magazines, and the extra cost to advertisers is small when particular pages or spaces are reserved for single, standard spot colour over-printing. If an advertiser requires spot colour on a page where it would not normally be available, or a particular colour which is not readily available, the cost is higher, since arrangements have to be made to print the additional colour on a page which would otherwise need to go only once through a printing unit on the press or, for special colours if special inks are needed.

It is sometimes feasible for spot, and even process colour (see p 99), to be introduced economically by 'picking up' colour from neighbouring pages. Publications are printed in sections, and if a section comprising several pages includes a page in colour it is practicable, with some forward planning, to print additional colour pages in that section in a single pass through the press, though in this case the choice of colour(s) is confined to those already in use elsewhere in that section.

Spot colour can be used creatively if basic principles are observed. One is that brilliant ('saturated') colours stand out and look more striking than pale (pastel) colours or tints. Some colours (eg yellow and light blue) are very weak when printed. Bold headlines, company names or logos, boldly drawn illustrations, headlines or devices and abstract geometrical shapes in colour can draw attention to an ad, but it is unwise to use colour for small type, or to emphasise single words. Fine line and halftone illustrations are also unsatisfactory when reproduced as spot colour on low-grade papers, such as newsprint.

Colour photography

Advertising photography is best left to professionals. Surprisingly, some advertisers fail to provide for photography in their advertising budgets and rely on finding something suitable when it is needed. This is short-sighted. Good photography is not expensive compared with other origination, and can make a significant contribution to the effectiveness of an advertisement. Photographs must play an active role in advertisements, and should never be used simply because nobody can think of anything better to fill a space. A photograph can make or break an ad, and a dull or out-of-scale one is worse than none at all. Run-of-the-mill photographs, much less amateur snapshots, are rarely if ever suitable for use in advertisements. Scale, impact, originality, relevance and optimum sharpness (definition) are important in advertising photography. A photograph must have visual impact and be capable of reproducing well.

Colour photographs may be either transparencies or positive prints. The former give the best printed results, though it is not easy to crop them (ie mechanically to eliminate any areas which are not required). Sharpness (definition), contrast, grain, density (colour saturation) and freedom from blemishes all contribute to good printed reproduction. All colour photographs lose definition the more they are enlarged and, for big enlargements (an A4 page or larger), 5 x 4 originals are preferable.

Pre-press and printing processes can have a far-reaching effect on colour fidelity and many controls are needed to match and adjust colours for reproduction. Only proofed or finished work can be assessed by the printers' customers and it is at the proofing stage that an evaluation must be made.

Briefing professional commercial photographers is straightforward provided you tell them the exact purpose for which a photograph will be used and ensure that a sufficient number is taken to allow a reasonably wide choice. Be prepared to provide any assistance or facilities that photographers may need to set up and light the subject.

Colour photographs, especially transparencies, are easily marred. Careful handling, protection and storage is essential. Photographic prints should not be mounted and should be protected against damage in transit. Identification is important, but avoid writing directly on the back of prints or on transparency mounts.

Process colour

Process colour allows a very wide range of colours in photographs and artwork to be reproduced in print. Supplying colour originals and artwork, and checking colour proofs, are the main in-house requirements. If there is a large throughput of colour advertising, computer-assisted design and colour origination systems may be employed, but these are far too complicated and expensive to be installed in-house by the majority of advertisers, though some printers, repro houses, professional designers and advertising agencies use them. If they do they will explain in detail whether their clients can benefit from them.

Colours are never absolutely identical to the originals after printing. As well as the conditions imposed by the technical requirements of reproduction and printing, paper surface and 'whiteness' (reflectance) have a direct influence on the fidelity of printed colour. Porous papers absorb printing ink, and are usually neither particularly white nor reflective, which makes the colours printed on them appear dingy when compared with the smoothness, opacity and reflectance of coated ('art') papers. Absorbent, low-reflectance papers, such as newsprint, cannot reproduce the tonal scale and brilliance obtainable on coated papers.

The question can therefore arise as to whether a particular medium is suitable for high-quality colour advertising, which may be costly to originate, and demand high-fidelity reproduction in print. In press advertising the advertiser cannot choose the paper on which an ad will be printed, so look carefully and critically at how other colour advertising appears in the proposed publication and decide whether it is up to the standard you will require. To do so some basic technical advice or knowledge is needed.

CHAPTER 11
Origination and Production

Camera-ready copy

Copy is said to be 'camera ready' when typesetting and layout is complete and can go forward for printing without further alteration or correction. For many purposes this is the best way of supplying laid-out text, since the advertisement can be examined as it will appear when printed. There are two straightforward ways of obtaining crc: directly from a photo-typesetting machine as positive or negative film or paper, or photographed from a montage on paper or board (camera-ready make-up). The former is by far the easier. Type has to be laid out before it can be printed, and this can be done entirely by the compositor (typesetter) if no instructions are given to the contrary. Most printers and publishers can be relied upon to work to acceptable typographical standards which are suited to the style and content of the end-product. If the advertiser is uncertain about type selection and layout and has no particular requirements, it is probably safer, and certainly easier, to leave it to someone who does.

Nevertheless, creative control over the final appearance of a printed text is preferable to 'what you see is what you get'. Typography and layout which is technically correct can still be typographically dreary, or simply undistinguished. Further-more, you have – or should have – a better idea of how you would like an ad to be presented, and what you want to achieve with it, than anyone else. An intelligent, observant and self-critical approach can, without a high level of typographical expertise, produce acceptable crc for publications and straightforward promotional printing, and a simple, well thought-out typographical mark-up alone can indicate fairly precisely how an ad could be typeset.

Before crc is undertaken it is essential to establish:

1. Whether it would be acceptable, and if so . . .
2. In what form it should be made available (how it should be presented).
3. When, and where, it must be forwarded for production.

For all practical purposes, phototypeset crc in the form of a single piece of positive or negative film, or printed on photographic paper, is its own 'proof': if it's not what's required it is still possible to alter it, but this is really a waste of time and money and not the object of the exercise: crc must eventually be *exactly* what is to appear in print.

It is possible to incorporate simple graphics, such as a logo, borders, typographical devices and simple line work at the typesetting stage for output as crc, but unusual typefaces and layouts, drawn and transfer lettering, photographs and line and tone artwork which cannot be handled by the phototypesetter will require a camera-ready layout to be produced.

There are, in my opinion, few advantages in presenting crc as camera-ready layout in the form of a flat and mounted montage except by professional studios and advertising production departments where resources are available and there is a large throughput of crc. The demands on studio skills, materials and techniques in this respect can be quite high. If studio facilities and skills are not available in-house they can, of course, be commissioned.

In this context a distinction must be made between crc which is made up mainly or entirely of composed text, headlines and typographical elements, and camera-ready artwork (see p 104).

Desktop publishing

Some mention can be made here of computer-based systems –

so-called desktop publishing (DTP) systems – which offer a wide range of computerised options for originating typesetting and page make-up via program packages and under operator control. DTP has advanced to a stage where elaborately finished page layouts, even ones which contain both text and graphics, can be produced entirely at a suitably equipped and programmed terminal. However, it should always be remembered that the means for converting DTP output into the required number of copies by a designated medium – in short printing it – will be needed, which is why the 'P' in DTP is deceptive! I have written thousands of words about DTP for trade and technical journals and talked to many seminars about its pros and cons, but the bottom line for DTP remains: it's not what it *can* do, but how efficiently, effectively and economically it is used in a given situation.

DTP systems are, for most publishing applications, slower and less versatile than advanced phototypesetters (which are, of course, also computer-based), and work to different operational parameters. The programmed capability of DTP in selecting and arranging type, manipulating graphics and outputting a printout is formidable but it does not include the technical knowledge, judgement and design skills needed to do everything properly, let alone satisfactorily. DTP operators should possess, or have direct access to, design and typographical skills as well as being competent and able to optimise the equipment's programmed potential.

Such comprehensive experience is hard to find, and training in the technical and aesthetic aspects of creating DTP output to professional print standards is thin on the ground. This said – and with the preconditions already mentioned – DTP has found useful applications, including the preparation of crc via laser printer output. If a DTP system is already installed it should not take long to find out whether it could be used to create crc; but if in-house DTP is envisaged solely or mainly for this purpose careful investigation is indicated, otherwise it could mean buying an expensive and unwieldy sledgehammer to crack this particular nut.

Of more general utility are word-processing systems, now widely used in commercial offices. They cannot output crc, but can be put to effective use in drafting, revising and arranging copy so that it reaches a fairly advanced stage before typesetting is commenced. This saves time, and can save money on corrections and alterations.

Camera-ready artwork

Camera-ready artwork shares many of the conditions already stated for camera-ready copy and layout. It also must be capable of being scaled and reproduced as presented, and in correct spatial relationships with other elements in the completed design. Small, relatively simple, single-colour items, such as company logos and line drawings, or hand-drawn lettering, are easily reproduced, enlarged or reduced by good quality photocopying, though remember that cra must be free of blemishes. Pins, staples, paper clips, sticky tape and anything else which makes marks are out! Instructions should be written on attached overlays, which also protect the surface of the artwork, and not on the actual artwork. Photocopies of cra should be taken for reference. Whether commissioned or internally created, the techniques required to produce cra, together with its exact size and scale and the printing process which will be used to reproduce it, should be known and understood by the artist or designer before work is commenced.

Line originals should be drawn in dense black inks, and may be larger than the size required for reproduction to improve definition and minimise any slight inaccuracies. Exact size for reproduction must, however, be shown on the overlay in terms of percentage enlargement or reduction, or by a linear measurement. If artwork or photographs are to be printed the same size as they are produced they should be marked 's/s' (same size). If artwork is intended as a 'spread', ie covering more than one page when printed, the position of margins and the fold ('gutter') must be taken into account.

The exact area to be reproduced should be indicated on photographs. If a photograph needs to be cropped a diagonal line from corner to corner, with vertical and horizontal lines on its x and y axes, will show the area to be reproduced and the area to be cropped. Retouching, if needed, should be done professionally. It is as well to remember that, unless otherwise instructed, the repro house will usually assume that a colour transparency should be reproduced as it stands.

Bleed (any image or solid which reaches the outside edges of a page when printed) must be indicated for correct trimming. Tints can be laid by the artist or inserted at the repro stage, which is more expensive but less fiddly.

Artwork should be mounted on stable board, though if it is to be processed by an electronic scanner it may be necessary for it to be detachable from its mount, or flexible enough to wrap around the drum of the machine.

Action guide

NOTE. This guide applies only to the preparation of camera-ready copy and artwork for single pages of monochrome and spot colour. Duotone and process colour cra requirements differ. For multi-page documents, printers' page impositions (the sequence in which pages are arranged during printing so that they will be presented in their correct order for folding, trimming and binding) vary and it could be difficult, or impossible, to impose the crc or artwork unless it is presented in the correct page sequence. In these circumstances it is essential to consult the repro house or printer who will be handling the job before preparing crc.

- If artwork is mounted it should be on a firm base to avoid the possibility of stuck-down copy coming loose if the base is flexed. For most jobs CS10 board is suitable for mounting but naturally this should not be used when the crc is supplied as typeset bromides (film).
- Non-image areas should consist of a plain white background extending to just beyond the required size of artwork to leave room for trim, centre, corner and fold marks.

- When black-and-white electronic scanners will *not* be used at the repro stage, positioning grids (guidelines) and instructions may be drawn on the artwork with pale blue ink or a chinagraph pencil. If a black-and-white scanner is to be used grids must not appear on artwork since these scanners are sensitive to blue and the grid lines would be reproduced. It is usually best to use overlays (covering sheets attached to the artwork) on mounted artwork and to write comments and instructions on these. For bromides, comments and instructions can be written on the envelope which protects the bromide (but take the bromide out of the envelope first!).

- Drawn artwork should be in good quality draughting ink, and free from marks and blemishes. Corrections should be impossible to see when reproduced photographically.

- If corrections are required after a bromide has been produced as crc the whole of the corrected section should be reset rather than stripping in (inserting) single words or lines to make a correction.

- Bromides of typesetting from phototypesetting machines should be correctly exposed, sharp, clean and of even density.

- Phototypeset copy must be secured firmly to the base of camera-ready layout. For this, solvent-based spray adhesives are more effective than waxes, except where there is a possibility of the solvent contaminating non-image-bearing areas.

- When combining drawn artwork and text avoid creating more than a single layer (a 'sandwich') on the upper surface of the base or carrier. This could become visible after photographing as unwanted edge lines, or create problems in focusing the artwork for reproduction.

- Logos should be made available as line artwork rather than line and tone or halftones (screened photographs).

- Artwork containing keylines for mechanical tint laying must include full instructions on its overlay, including all tint values for each section where tints are required.

- Illustrations supplied separately from the crc must indicate clearly on their overlay sheets where they belong, giving their exact sizes and positions together with any special instructions, eg for cutouts, vignettes, etc.
- When halftone illustrations are used, liaise with the printer so that their densities can be adjusted in relation to other parts of the artwork in the crc. The best results are obtained when halftones are stripped in.
- Photographs which have already been screened for printing will produce interference effects (moiré) if incorporated into crc and screened a second time. Printed photographs should not be used if any alternative is available, but if they are, the crc in which they are incorporated should always be supplied s/s (same size).
- Do not handle bromides, or leave them exposed to dust or heat.
- Give yourself all the time you need: rushed crc is fraught with dangers.
- Work cleanly and with good materials. Inspect crc carefully, using a magnifier.
- Never guess. If you're not sure about something consult someone who is.

CHAPTER 12
Print Buying

Print is at the sharp end of your advertising. A lack of confidence in organising and ordering print can cause companies to fight shy of print-based media such as brochures, sales letters, direct mail and point-of-sale display, so now is the time to review not only your advertising print but also your everyday print requirements such as letterheads, invoices, price-lists and packaging. Call on whatever skilled advice and assistance you need (and can afford), go cautiously and work within your budget. The results will be worth the effort.

Nobody expects to get what they want from a supermarket simply by asking for 'some groceries'; yet printers are frequently required to interpret equally vague specifications. A book could be written about how to buy print (in fact I have written one: *Print Buying*, David & Charles, 1986). Here I will deal with basics. To buy print you must:

- Decide what's wanted.
- Specify it.
- Find someone who can supply it.
- Provide whatever is necessary to produce it.

Whether these preconditions are met by an advertising agency, a professional print buyer or the reader of this book, they must somehow be fulfilled. For some print jobs that might not be difficult; but remember that before anything can be printed it has to be specified and originated. Printing costs cannot be estimated accurately without a clear idea of what is wanted in print on paper (and, by the way, the paper can often cost more than the printing!).

Specifying

To specify print you need to know what will be needed to produce it as planned. Apart from origination – copy, artwork, layout, etc – papers, repro, typesetting, finishing (eg trimming, folding, stitching and binding) and post-print requirements, such as inserting and delivery, must also be specified. If you don't do it somebody else has to.

A specification should also state whether origination (everything the printer needs to have in hand before the job can be printed) will be supplied by the customer, an advertising agency or through trade services such as typesetters, repro houses, etc.

If it is found to be impracticable or too expensive to produce what is specified, the customer has three choices: alter the specification, look for another printer or abandon the specification.

It is a good idea to use a pro forma specification for each job as it arises. Anything not needed can be left out, but the standardised specification form will safeguard against leaving anything out which ought to be there. A pro forma specification should include at least the following data:

- Length of run (the number of printed products required)
- Number of pages and overall dimensions
- Typography and layout instructions
- Paper and board specifications
- Typesetting and repro requirements
- Number of proofs required
- Binding or finishing requirements
- Names and addresses of outside suppliers, eg of design, artwork, typesetting or photography
- Directions and date(s) for delivery or despatch.

The printer will eventually need to know:

- In what form, by whom and when origination (copy, photographs, typesetting, mark-up, camera-ready copy, layout and artwork) will be supplied.
- When, and in what form, any address lists needed for despatch will be available.

Some of these details may have to be decided after the job is placed, since they are based not on the specification but on a production schedule. It will probably not be possible to include all of them in an initial specification, but the aim is to produce as detailed and accurate a specification as you can.

Before placing an order, it is sensible to ascertain precisely what you stand to get for what you pay. Such things as the number of proofs required, how corrections will be handled and charged, whether delivery costs are included in the quoted price and whether there is a cost penalty for failing to meet origination deadlines should be established. Know the conditions of trading – read the 'small print' in the contract – before signing orders. If trade services will be needed the production schedule must be organised to allow for them: moving materials and partly processed print from one place to another takes time, which the production schedule must allow for if processing is carried out in separate locations.

Run-length should be estimated carefully. The shorter the run, the higher the unit cost, though this should not encourage over-ordering 'to be on the safe side'. It is economical and time-saving to ask the printer to retain origination if a subsequent printing is anticipated. Reprinting can then be done quickly and without the need to respecify and set up the same job all over again. Reprints of items with standard formats, such as price-lists, which are called off regularly and are subject to few changes, can be updated quickly in-house, re-ordered and reprinted with minimum fuss. For most jobs it is prudent to obtain a run-on price from the printer (which, since it does not include pre-press costs, will be lower per printed unit than for the original run) so that, either immediately or in the reasonably near future, a further run can be ordered.

Finding a printer

The printer you know, especially the one with experience of your company's print needs, should be your first port of call. While it should never be assumed that a printer who has already done a particular job satisfactorily can tackle others equally well, existing relationships are valuable.

If they are any good, printers and their reps are able to offer technical information and practical advice, which is free and worth having, especially in helping to decide whether the specification is appropriate to what's wanted, and can be met. Consultation with printers, typesetters and other suppliers before a job is placed may also save money: small, apparently unimportant, changes can make a material difference to whether what is specified can be produced economically and satisfactorily. With or without such alterations, the final specification is what the printer undertakes to supply.

Professional print buyers maintain a 'panel' of printers, services and suppliers who they know from experience will respond promptly and efficiently to enquiries and give good service, but even if you have no direct experience of printers it is not always necessary to obtain several estimates for a job, unless it is an unfamiliar or particularly complicated one, or unless price is of overriding importance. If more than one estimate is required make sure that every estimate obtained is based on the same specification.

Keep a file of printed specimens (a 'job bag') of every completed job, together with estimates, job specifications and final invoices. These provide the information you need to build up your printers 'panel'. Print buying is 'horses for courses'. If a wide range of print is used the buyer must also be prepared to keep a close eye on market changes, especially paper prices, and to consider new, as well as existing, suppliers.

Franchised chains of high street printshops and specialised trade houses (or bureaux) offer packaged, but often quite comprehensive, services for well-defined print needs, often with ancillary services such as design, typesetting and repro as well as printing. If such packages contain what's wanted they are easy to cost and buy.

'Bespoke' (commercial) printers may offer additional specialised services under one roof, or be able to buy them in for their customers. Dealing with a single supplier has obvious advantages though, nowadays, this might not be possible. Some printers are equipped with the machinery and expertise needed to specialise in particular market sectors, such as point-of-sale print and direct mail; others are more versatile. In all cases the work must be fitted to the machinery and equipment available to produce it. This includes not only printing presses but also pre-press systems, such as colour scanners and phototypesetters, and any bindery or finishing necessary to complete the job.

It is the customer's responsibility to ensure that all origination is present and correct when it is needed. Finding out what will be necessary before the job can be produced as specified is best tackled by early liaison with printers and suppliers. After you and your supplier have agreed about what's wanted a production schedule can be prepared (see p 114).

Size, format, length of run, materials, pre-press and finishing requirements can all affect how efficiently and economically a job can be produced. For example, large web-offset presses are fast and have useful in-line options such as folding, but can only be used efficiently and economically in a range of specified formats and run-lengths. Other reel-fed and sheet-fed presses are better suited to irregular formats and shorter runs. Printers equipped for one kind of work will not readily accept orders for a job outside their chosen market. If, for any reason, they do, their prices may reflect this unwillingness!

Offset litho is the main printing process used for monochrome or colour. Other processes, such as embossing, screen process printing and packaging, require special equipment and expertise which is available from specialists in these particular fields.

One thing is certain: whatever you want will have to be paid for. Planning and designing print without reference to what it could cost to produce is futile. Over-elaboration, over-ordering and underestimating production requirements lead to expense, frustration and, ultimately, to a disenchantment with print and printers.

The production schedule

A production schedule is a timetable showing exactly when each operation should be started, completed and delivered in accordance with the media schedule (see pp 18–20). If, for any reason, the media schedule is changed the production schedule will also need to be changed.

A 'master' production schedule shows the estimated time needed fully to complete each creative and production requirement. For this a wall chart planner can be used, which is easily adapted to your particular needs and methods of working. This will give a panoramic 'picture' of all planned and scheduled advertising, and can be amended and updated as required.

Separate, more detailed production schedules based on this 'master' schedule will be needed for individual projects where several stages of preparation are involved: design, copywriting, artwork, printing, finishing, etc. The aim is to make the exact amount of time required for *all* time-consuming operations clear and highly visible for each advertising project to whoever controls it, and to anyone else who needs to know. Deadlines for design, copy, artwork, repro, printing, etc can then be fixed, correlated and made realistic.

In press advertising copy deadlines are sacrosanct: if you miss them your advertisement will not appear when you want it to, and you may also incur financial penalties (see p 35). Sales letters and print, such as brochures and direct mail, which are originated in-house but produced elsewhere, should be tightly scheduled from start to finish. It is fatally easy to underestimate how long it takes to discuss, prepare and produce what's wanted when it's wanted. Exhibition requirements (see pp 71–3) in particular can fall foul of late and imperfect scheduling. Last-minute scrambles are a recipe for disaster.

Non-production requirements which take time to complete, such as origination, delivery and transportation, must be taken into account in making a production schedule if it is to work smoothly.

Individual production schedules are best divided chronologically into a sequence corresponding to the progress of the job, eg origination, production and forwarding and, where necessary, distribution, remembering that a schedule cannot dictate what *will* happen – only what *ought* to happen. It is obviously not sensible to schedule anything which requires printing for distribution before it is known how long it will take to print. Press ads cannot appear until they are created and forwarded for publication; but experience (which indicates when and where delays are likely to occur) plus a certain amount of blind faith are needed to produce a convincing production schedule. Take account of time-consuming peripheral activities such as meetings, discussions, creative or administrative 'thinking time', briefing and liaison, and in-house requirements such as copywriting, proof-reading and colour correction. The aim is to schedule realistically, but not inflexibly.

Any time taken up in postal delivery, travel and transportation, courier services, obtaining materials such as envelopes, paper or folders, or public holidays, can upset an apparently workable schedule if not taken into account when making it. If you simply don't know how long a particular requirement is likely to take don't guess – ask. An outside service or supplier who cannot, or will not, say how long it will take to carry out properly specified work – and stick to it – is not worth dealing with. Tell people what is expected of them; they will respond better to clear instructions than to vague and imprecise requests.

Be reasonable. You are not the only one involved. You may think that he who pays the piper has the right to call the tune, but if insufficient time is allowed for people to work at a reasonable pace you risk losing part of what you're paying for.

Finally, do not be lulled into a sense of false security by 'new technology'. However speedy automated production equipment may seem, in printing its potential is realised only by the people who use it. Remember that this year's model doesn't move any quicker than last year's in a traffic jam!

If, for any reason, the schedule has to be changed, guard against a knock-on effect which could reduce the time available to complete the whole job properly and without rush or panic. To make every job a rush job is inconsiderate, to say nothing of living dangerously.

Action guide

- Make a 'master' displayed production schedule, and produce separate schedules for each advertising project.
- Gear the schedule to the job specification. When instructing and briefing suppliers, say not only what's wanted, but also when you want it produced as specified.
- Check dates for overlap. Whenever possible, build safety margins into the production schedule.
- Do not say you want things earlier than you really do 'just to be on the safe side'. Your schedule should be believable and workable.
- If the schedule is upset make sure that you know immediately it happens, how it happened and where it has happened. Rescue it if you can, preferably *before* throwing a fit of temperament!

Making complaints

People are involved in producing print, and Murphy's Law intrudes at every stage. When clear, precise instructions have been given what can be done when things have gone irretrievably wrong? Well, you complain; but first make sure of three things: that it wasn't your fault; that your complaint is on firm grounds; that it is directed to the right quarter. Delays and incorrect quantities are easy to discover, usually when it's too late to do much about them. Technical defects and shortcomings are harder to pin down. It can be difficult to establish with certainty what has caused an unacceptable printed result – it could be paper, inks, drying, machining, finishing operations and a host of other things. Whatever caused the problem it's an even chance that the buck will be passed.

Copies of the job specification and the production schedule for every job should have been filed. Letters, contracts, confirmations, memos and written instructions relating to the job, or the placement of an ad, may also be relevant in establishing the cause of a dispute and settling it.

If, despite your best efforts, results fall seriously short of expectations, little is achieved by immediately throwing a tantrum. On the other hand, you deserve to get what you pay for, and if you think you haven't, try to establish not only how but also where things went awry, and what steps might be necessary to prevent it happening again.

Gross defects, such as reversed or misplaced illustrations or captions, should be detected in proof. The gremlins which can strike during repro, platemaking and machining, or because of incorrect or inappropriate papers, are harder to pin down. Conspicuous colour defects, blemishes and paper damage can be caused before, during or after printing, eg in storage or during transportation. First check whether a visible defect is present throughout the run, or is confined to only a few copies. If not, investigate. Suppliers, and the advertising media, need your custom and, provided your specification was complete and your complaint cogent and reasonable, they will usually do everything possible to keep it, even if it means re-running a job or reprinting an ad in a subsequent issue without cost.

This being so, do not become a chronic complainer: your suppliers and the media are on your side! Do some homework on paper and printing technology so that you can talk the same language as the people you deal with so that your instructions are understood and can be followed correctly.

CHAPTER 13
Testing

If you have no way of measuring how effective your advertising is there is no way of being sure whether it is worth what you are paying for it or, if not, how it could be improved. Advertising itself does not make a profit; on the contrary it costs money. What it produces in terms of added sales can only be assessed on results.

It would be convenient if, by subtracting advertising expenditure from profits over a given period, it were possible to show exactly how much profit could be attributed to advertisements; but that is not possible except, perhaps, when *all* sales can be attributed to advertisements, for example in off-the-page selling, and for some forms of direct mail.

For most advertising it takes time and patience to assess whether the effort put into it is achieving what is intended. There are reasons for advertising other than to produce immediate sales – recruitment, dealer information, 'prestige' advertising and sales-force support for example – but if advertising is not undertaken with the intention of improving a company's trading in the longer or shorter term, and in some measurable way, it is hard to see what value it could have.

The only reliable test is to measure and evaluate response. There is, of course, no certainty that everybody who responds to an ad becomes a customer, but response accurately assesses the pulling power of your advertising. Also, it is possible to relate the response rate to a sales increase only when advertising has been monitored. Direct mail (see p 39) uses customer identification techniques which can easily be adapted to display advertising. For example, ads which contain reply coupons which offer readers something, such as a brochure, booklet, sample or price-list, can establish how many readers of the advertisement were prepared not only to read the ad but also to take action on it.

Naturally, there is no guarantee that such respondents become buyers, nor is this level of response unchallengeable evidence of an ad's *selling* power, though it certainly identifies potential customers and improves the conversion rate.

Some magazines include bound-in response cards which encourage readers to request further information from advertisers. If these are processed promptly and efficiently by the magazine's advertising department (which isn't always the case) they can be used as a measure of advertising response, as well as for sales leads.

It is worth considering responses other than coupon-clipping if they could provide some useful feedback. For example, a manufacturer of private telephone exchanges suggests in its advertising that readers call their own offices, and 'if the phone rings more than three times, hang up and call us!' Such ingenious ideas are well worth inventing, since all verifiable response is valuable.

Testing of this kind is closely related to the content, particularly the copy element, of an ad. All ads seek some kind of response, but not all response can easily be measured. Some advertisers undertake or commission customer or reader research to obtain information which can be used to improve their advertising. For large, ongoing campaigns this can be valuable, but careful thought should be given before mounting research of this kind through questionnaires and surveys. To be of real value it has to be conducted skilfully. Standard questionnaires need to be carefully framed and analysed, and expertly interpreted. They can also be costly to administer professionally, and if done unprofessionally can be unrepresentative when people answer your questions carelessly, or do not answer them at all owing to lack of clear, unambiguous instructions. Companies which handle their own advertising are better advised to be alert to whatever testing opportunities are feasible.

It is certainly worthwhile introducing internal procedures which could help to establish how people react to your advertising, and whether any enquiries or calls you receive were made as a direct result of it. Some members of a company's staff, in particular its sales force, are well placed to do this and should be made aware of the importance of finding out as much as possible in-house, and in the field, about its advertising. Is it read? Is it considered informative? Can customers and potential customers remember it? Have they responded to a particular ad? If so, where did they see it? Correlate, classify, study and interpret this information – it is valuable for response testing because it is directly related to your business.

Testing of a different kind is possible when a direct response (couponed) ad is placed in more than one journal. A simple printed code on the coupon allows the advertiser to relate response to specific exposures. This kind of information can be put to good use in many ways, especially in planning future advertising.

Response analysis also plays an important part in media selection (see pp 21–3). Simply counting advertising leads is not enough to indicate whether you are using the most cost-effective media; you also need to know where the leads come from. An ad which reaches a million people will probably cost more than one which reaches 2000. A 2 per cent response from the former would be 200,000, while a 2 per cent response from the latter would be 400. Which are you looking for? The higher exposure figure will not necessarily produce more conversions: it depends on what you are selling, the quality of your advertising and your sales back-up.

'Below the line' advertising – which is not media-based (like press and TV advertising) but is initiated and progressed by the advertiser in-house, or by an agency, (eg printed brochures, circulars and catalogues) – can be difficult to test in any depth, though it is worth devising methods of getting at least some useful information from it. A unique reference number or code, quoted by a customer when making an enquiry or placing an order, allows such enquiries or orders easily to be traced to specific sources, such as particular brochures or catalogues. What is often done less efficiently is making sure that any information obtained in this way is applied, interpreted and used to identify successful formulae and capitalise on them, and in the case of less successful projects to improve them, eg by making design, copywriting, production or distribution changes. If sales records, order forms, invoicing and similar commercial data carry some source identification in order to process them it should not take a Sherlock Holmes to make useful deductions about where orders stem from and which are likely to be the result of advertising response.

Action guide

- Test primary response rather than conversion rates in press advertising, or fulfilment in direct mail, however and whenever possible.
- Test all media and exposures, and below-the-line advertising, over comparable periods. Remember that response can vary seasonally, geographically and in other important ways, so test over longer rather than shorter periods.
- Vary your advertising approach and test to establish which ads are pulling best.
- Use reader-response cards when available, file them (after following them up!) and analyse response by magazine, date of insertion, advertisement, number of reader enquiries received and, if applicable, conversion rate.

Further Information

Further reading from Kogan Page

Commonsense Direct Marketing, Drayton Bird, 2nd edn, 1989
A Handbook of Advertising Techniques, Tony Harrison, 2nd edn, 1989
How to Increase Sales Without Leaving Your Desk, Edmund Tirbutt, 1991
How to Make Exhibitions Work for Your Business, John Talbot, 1989
How to Market Books, Alison Baverstock, 1990
Readymade Business Letters, Jim Dening, 1988
Readymade Job Advertisements, Neil Wenborn, 1991
Running a Successful Advertising Campaign, Iain Maitland, 1989
Sales Promotion, Julian Cummins, 1989
Successful Exhibiting, James W Dudley, 1990
Successful Marketing for the Small Business, Dave Patten, 2nd edn, 1988

Useful addresses

Advertising Standards Authority
Brook House, 2–16 Torrington Place, London WC1E 7HN;
071-580 5555

The Association of Mail Order Publishers
1 New Burlington Street, London W1X 1FD;
071-437 0706

Audit Bureau of Circulations (ABC)
13 Wimpole Street, London W1M 7AB;
071-631 1343

Code of Advertising Practice Committee
Brook House, 2–16 Torrington Place, London WC1E 7HN;
071-580 5555

Mailing Preference Service
26 Eccleston Street, London SW1W 9PY;
071-730 0844

Mail Order Publishers' Authority
1 New Burlington Street, London W1X 1FD;
071-437 0706

Marketing Week
St Giles House, 50 Poland Street, London W1V 4AX;
071-439 4222

National Consumer Council
20 Grosvenor Gardens, London SW1W 0DH;
071-730 3469